LOOKING FOR COUNTRY
A NORWEGIAN IMMIGRANT'S ALBERTA MEMOIR

Ellenor Ranghild Merriken

Introduction by Janice Dickin

University of Calgary Press

University of Calgary Press,
2500 University Drive N.W.
Calgary, Alberta, Canada T2N 1N4

Canadian Cataloguing in Publication Data

Merriken, Ellenor R. (Ellenor Ranghild), 1899-1990
    Looking for country

    (Legacies shared)
    Previous ed. has title: The Nose Hills country.
    Includes bibliographical references and index.
    ISBN 1-55238-007-6

    1. Merriken, Ellenor R. (Ellenor Ranghild), 1899-1990 2. Frontier and pioneer life--Alberta--
Nose Hill Region (Coronation). 3. Women pioneers--Alberta--Nose Hill Region (Coronation)
--Biography. 4. Norwegians--Alberta--Nose Hill Region (Coronation)--Biography. 5. Nose Hill
Region (Coronation, Alta.)--Biography. I. Title. II. Title: Nose Hills country. III. Series.
FC3695.N692Z49 1999   971.23'3   C99-910552-3
F1079.N67M47 1999

Canada [*] We acknowledge the financial support of the Government of Canada through the
Book Publishing Industry Development Program (BPIDP) for our publishing activities.

The Alberta
Foundation
for the Arts

Publication and promotion of this book has been made
possible by financial assistance from the
Alberta Foundation for the Arts.

COMMITTED TO THE DEVELOPMENT OF CULTURE AND THE ARTS

Printed and bound in Canada by Veilleux Impression à Demande Inc.

∞ This book is printed on acid-free paper.

Cover and book design by Glitch Graphics.
*Cover: Photographs from family collection. Background: Big Gap Stampede, Neutral Hills, 1917. Inset:
Ellenor at family gathering, ca. mid-1920s.*

Series Preface

This volume is part of the Legacies Shared series. The aim of the series is to publish material that either has never been published or is out of print.

The mandate of Legacies Shared is broad, as we plan to make available parts of our "legacy" of historical memories that have been overlooked or have disappeared. Each volume contains an introduction appropriate to the subject, which might be a work of history, a memoir, collections of letters, photographs, art work, maps or recipes, works of fiction or poetry, or sets of archival documents. Oral history will also have a place in the series.

The geographical area covered by this series is the Canadian west and north, but also across the Canada/U.S. border.

Janice Dickin, Series Editor,
Professor, Faculty of General Studies,
University of Calgary, Alberta

Acknowledgements   *Janice Dickin*

Many people helped with this book. I want to thank in particular Jean Merriken Andrew, who made available not only her time but family lore, photos and documents. Also of great help was Dorothy Kelts, the daughter of Martin Olsen, Jr. Sadly, Dorothy died before the manuscript found its home with the University of Calgary Press. I also want to thank Gerry Hallowell, who made useful editorial suggestions, and the various anonymous readers, all of whom helped to evaluate and improve my introduction. The staff at University of Calgary Press, especially Walter Hildebrandt, have been generous with advice and assistance. I would also like to thank Joan Eadie for compiling the index. Finally, thanks to Elspeth Cameron, who participated in a research trip to Veteran and Consort and who helped me in countless other ways.

For my father,
Gordon Clark Dickin,
the son and grandson of pioneers

Introduction — *Janice Dickin*

On the island of Karmoy, near the town of Skudneshaven, in the jurisdiction of Rogaland, in the northern nation of Norway, there lived at the turn of the century a farming-fishing-professional family. The parents had met and married in the American mid-west. The oldest child had been born in Kansas. The father repeatedly returned to seek his fortune in the New World. One day, early in 1910, the family sold up or packed up everything they owned and sailed from the nearby port of Stavanger, en route to the prairies of east-central Alberta. Although Norwegian names are given differently, the family became known in their new home by the name of Olsen. Ellenor Ranghild Merriken, the author of this memoir, was the youngest daughter of the Olsen family.

The expression "looking for country" is used to approximate the thought process of animals bent on escape. A stampeding herd may be described as "looking for country", as may a spooked horse running away with its rider. It is an expression that Ellenor Merriken used. But there are other ways to read the phrase, ways that can be applied to this memoir. In emigrating, the Olsen family was following the lead of their patriarch and of many other Europeans in looking for land, a piece of a new country. While some actively sought to escape the old ways, others found themselves inadvertently "freed" from customs and comforts they thought—wrongly—they would be able to reproduce in this new country. For such people, emigration could bring great sadness. Ellenor was not one of these. She loved Alberta and took tremendous pride in the years she spent there as a pioneer. She did not deny the struggles but felt them amply rewarded by "the satisfaction of knowing that I have had a part in the making of a great country." [1]

Her own sadness would blossom upon emigration to the eastern United States more than two decades later. Still a young woman, she felt forced to leave, to accompany her ailing husband to his old country, Maryland. As she struggled to re-settle in a cultural and social climate she felt confining, she looked back to Alberta with longing, promising herself that she would return. She never did, though she held onto the land for almost four more decades, visiting whenever she could, proud that she could still sit a saddlehorse, glad for a gallop across the prairie. Over the last thirty years of her life, she looked back to write this memoir (originally self-published as *The Nose Hills Country*) as well as a number of other glimpses at the Alberta countryside she loved. This introduction to this new edition seeks to provide biographical material she did not include; to set her life in the context of Norwegian emigration, particularly to Alberta; and to discuss her life as a writer.

The story of how the Olsens came to the Alberta prairie is both similar to and different from the stories of countless other immigrants. Apart from Ireland, Norway contributed a greater proportion of her population to the European cultural expansion of the nineteenth and early twentieth century than did any other nation.[2] Like Ireland, she became in this indirect way a colonial force. Although both countries have been considered backwaters in terms of European power and politics, they nonetheless were caught up in the dynamism of capitalism in the eighteenth and nineteenth centuries. Furthermore, partly because of their backwater status, they underwent stresses that could not be accommodated easily within their own borders. In the case of Norway, the stresses included a near tripling of population (from 883,000 in 1801 to 2,240,000 in 1901); a severe economic crisis following the Napoleonic Wars; then, economic recovery accomplished partly through centralizing systems of industrialization and transportation which destroyed the smaller centres.[3]

The villages strung out along Norway's fjords, especially in the north, could no longer support their own: the food-growers who could not rent land enough for their growing families, the flax-farmers whose prices were undercut by the easy import of cheap cotton, the shoemakers and cabinetmakers who could not match the economies of the urban factories, all had to consider moving. For those who wished to continue farming, there was nowhere to go in Norway itself. The land comprises 74% barren mountains, mountain lakes and glaciers; 23% forest; and only 3% cultivated meadows, natural meadows and grain fields.[4]

Once the decision was made to move, possible destinations were not limited to those in Norway itself. Although by 1891 only 8.58% of the population was working in the fisheries,[5] Norway had long been a sea-going nation, proud of its Viking past. Part of the country's economic recovery was accomplished through shipping and, by the end of the nineteenth century, tiny Norway had the third largest merchant navy in the world, after the United Kingdom and the United States. Norwegians were used to putting to sea. One group who did so were the "Sloopers", a group of 52 pietists[6] bent on escaping religious oppression. Like the Olsens, they hailed mostly from the rural communities of Rogaland and set sail for New York—in a 54 foot sloop, on 4 July 1825—from the same port of Stavanger. With help, they established a Norwegian beachhead on Lake Ontario in northern New York state which would serve as a way-station for later waves of immigrants.

Migration from Norway did not become an annual trend until 1836 but it soon gained momentum, becoming a mass exodus by the mid-1860s. Three major waves of emigration occurred between then and 1910, with only a few Norwegians leaving by the 1920s.[7] Not all emigrants left for good. There was always a steady backflow—after 1880, something in the nature of 25% [8]—usually young unmarried men who had emigrated to find work, not a new life. Restless Martin Olsen, Sr., Ellenor's father, contributed to the emigration statistics time and time again.

Between 1900 and 1914, almost 215,000 Norwegians left their homeland and, after 1905, the authorities thought to ask them why. Between 80% and 90% of the men said they left to find profitable employment; 60-75% of the women said the same. Some of these commitments to the New World were of such short duration that the emigres were really only "birds of passage", the equivalent of eastern Canadian harvest workers who went west yearly only for the threshing season. In one documented case, 80 fisherman from Skudneshavn on the island of Karmoy took part in the fisheries on the east coast of the United States in 1904 and then returned home for the next year's winter herring season.[9]

By the time the Olsens left Norway, family emigration complete with a string of children was no longer the norm. By the 1900s, nearly two-thirds of the emigrants were single men between the ages of 15 and 25.[10] As well, the Olsens differed from the earlier emigration of families in that they were not heading for the American midwest but for Canada, a country to which countless and uncounted Norwegians had set sail en route to the United States but in which Norwegian settlements had largely failed, starting with an attempt in Quebec in 1854.[11] The Olsens headed directly to Alberta, the province which would become the focal point for Norwegian population and heritage in Canada.[12]

By the time Ellenor and her family arrived in 1910, there was already an established Norwegian community in the east-central part of the province. Some of these settlers came directly from Norway but a large number were transplants from the American midwest: victims of drought, younger sons crowded off prosperous farms or simply people who pioneered as a business—taking homesteads, proving up, selling out and moving on.[13] One source makes it clear that, viewed from south of the border, this look to the Canadian prairie as new country was simply a seamless move to the "last agricultural frontier in the northwestward push of settlement."[14] Certainly Norwegians were not unusual in following their star north: in the first decade of the twentieth century, 44% of homestead entries made in western Canada were by immigrants from the United States.[15]

Canadian officials targeted Norwegians as particularly desirable immigrants for the new territories.[16] The prime reasons for this were notions of Nordic industriousness and assimilability held by the dominant Anglo-Canadian culture. In addition, the Norwegian settlers from the U.S. came complete with years of experience in dryland farming and it was in this quarter that the Canadian government had most success. Despite heavy recruitment in Norway itself, Canada could not compete with decades of "America letters," both personal and published, urging Norwegians still at home to join their compatriots in Minnesota, in Iowa, in Wisconsin, in Illinois, in the Dakotas. Although Canada did start to become a distinguishable destination for Norwegian emigration after 1900, it still received only 10% of those leaving between 1900 and 1914, the proportion increasing to 24% in the 1920s.[17]

Norwegian homesteaders coming to Alberta chose farm land in the new areas opening up within about a fifty mile radius of what is now the city of Camrose,[18] originally called Oslo, after the capital of Norway. By 1896, there existed a Norwegian settlement at Crooked Lake, northeast of Wetaskiwin.[19] On the western edge of the radius, near Olds, lies another early settlement. The five families and two single males who established Eagle Hill were all part of a group who had settled in 1885 in Minnesota, on bad land with swamp, sand ridges and rocks. After six years of clearing trees and picking rocks, they began seriously to look for better land. One man contacted a friend who had settled at Harmattan in what was still the North West Territories and got an enthusiastic reply. Three men came up to scout. They filed for homesteads and went home to sell up. The group arrived at its new home—a big rounded hill with only one other homesteader in sight—in June 1902. They threshed their first grain in 1903 and built their first school in 1906, allowing students as old as 20 to catch up on the education foregone as a result of the move. Bergen, a community with pietist origins, was established nearby in 1905 and Inverness, another largely Norwegian community, in 1906.[20]

By the time the Olsen family arrived, the land was filling in, good land inexorably available only farther and farther out from the main centres of population. Although Ellenor tells us that her father simply tossed a coin to decide between Canada and Australia, his decision was more likely based on a combination of his own familiarity with North America and the presence of two brothers in the Norwegian settlement of Bawlf, Alberta. So far as I can ascertain, the family had no contacts in Australia. Ellenor does not even mention the United States as an option; Martin, Sr. had already failed at least three times to gain a foothold there.

On 10 April 1910, Martin and Johana Olsen and their children Martha, Serina (Sina), Lillie, Ranghild (Ellenor) and the twins, Ole and Martin, lay seasick in the first class lounge of the *Rogaland*, crossing the choppy North Sea. Once in England, they took the train to Liverpool. Ellenor used to tell her children that her father pointed out to them there the *Titanic* under construction.[21] The tale is likely apocryphal but tells us much about how "ordinary" people feel compelled to order their life narratives around "extraordinary" events. The ship the Olsens took to the new world was the *Lake Champlain*, bound for Quebec City. From there, they took the transcontinental railway through the Shield and across the prairies. Weeks after they had started, they completed their journey in a lumber wagon under a full moon. They were taken to the home of Uncle Knud, a widower with five children. The oldest, Olga, 13, was waiting up with supper and a three layer cake.

The source for what led up to the cataclysmic and—for two of the family—fatal decision to resettle is not Ellenor but her older (by 9 years) sister Lillie who has also left us a memoir.[22] Another Norwegian-Albertan writer and memoirist, the Canadian diplomat Chester Ronning, tells a story of visiting his ancestral home in Norway and asking a distant relative still living there how the Ronning grandparents could have borne to leave such a lovely place. "Your grandparents", came the reply, "with a large family could not live on wild fruit and scenery."[23] While this was the experience of many, it does not appear from Lillie's memoir that economic exigency was the real drive behind the Olsen exodus. She paints a picture of a successful professional mother with the support of a comfortable family, educational opportunities and government connections. There was domestic conflict but there was no deprivation. Although the family, in essence, borrowed money to leave, there is no indication that they were forced out. Martin reputedly justified the move as necessary to get his late-born, longed-for twin sons away from the dangerous North Sea. It is also clear that, by this time, Martin had little attachment to the place of his birth and a fatal attraction to the New World.

Ellenor's parents, Martin Cornelius Olsen Liknes and Johana Maria Rasmussen Hemnes were both born in 1860[24] on the island of Karmoy. Both were 50 years old when they brought their family to Canada. Their lives, on the surface so connected, in reality were very different. It somehow comes as no surprise that there exists no family photo of the two of them together.

Martin Olsen was born the fifth child and fourth son in a family of eight.[25] In addition to his wages as a schoolteacher, Martin's father, Skule Ola, owned a farm on which the family grew its own food and raised sheep for wool. Skule Ola made their shoes and his wife their clothing.[26] Everything was passed down and Martin later told Ellenor that he never had a new pair of Sunday shoes till he bought them for himself. Whether or not Martin was inclined to continue in this subsistence style of living, he stood no chance of inheriting the land. At age 14, he signed on as cabin boy on a sailing ship carrying freight around the world. When he arrived home a year later, he gave his mother the meagre wages he had saved. For ten more years, Martin followed the sea, alternating cargo ships with fishing expeditions to the Grand Banks. Finally at age 25, he stepped off a ship in New York harbor and headed for Kansas to join two older brothers homesteading there.

Johana Hemnes was born the seventh of nine children on what Ellenor refers to as "the old family estate." The fact that Johana's family was in far better circumstances than was Martin's is evidenced by the fact that she spent six years studying nursing and medicine at the University of Bergen. She also learned English with an English accent that later amused her children. Adventurous in her own right, Johana set sail after graduation in 1886 to visit her sister Karina in Selina, Kansas. Karina

(Carrie in the United States) was married to Martin's older brother, Lars. Whatever previous knowledge they might have had of one another, Johana and Martin married 20 November 1887 and Johana went to live on Martin's new homestead.

Johana later led Ellenor to believe that she had been shocked to find Karina living in a sod hut which resembled the old potato cellars in Norway. It is therefore unclear why she chose to replicate her sister's experience. What is clear is that she did not try it for long. Two years of drought followed the wedding and Johana, with a new baby, longed for home. Martin left for the goldfields of California to earn money for her passage. It seems that Johana sailed for Norway alone with her daughter Martha. Perhaps Martin followed soon after or perhaps Johana was pregnant when she left: a second daughter, Serina, was born in Norway on 29 November 1889. We know that Martin did return by the end of 1890: a third daughter, Lillie, was born 28 October 1891. He was not, however, there for the birth. He left again for the States in September of that year. Lillie did not meet her father until 1898, when she was nearly seven. Years later, she wrote: "I don't think he could have been very impressed with me and as for me he was just a stranger."27 A fourth daughter, Ranghild (eventually renamed Ellenor by her own husband) was born within a year of Martin's return on 27 August 1899 and the twin boys, Martin and Ole, less than two years after that, on 10 August 1901. Ten months later, Martin was gone again, this time to Washington state to try the lumber business.

During Martin's long years of absence, Johana lived first with her parents, then—after her father's death and the birth of her third child—bought a little farm nearby. She supported her family from this land and from money she made as midwife and nurse. The government assigned her one third of the island as her exclusive territory and she worked hard at her job and at the farmwork, leaving her children in the care of a babysitter or of one another.

Lillie has left us a picture of this period which mixes descriptions of the golden days of childhood with clear signs of family conflict. While she had fond memories of the little farm with its cosy bungalow and orchard and playhouse, she bore deep resentment towards her absent father, her absorbed mother, her "prettier" older sisters and the younger siblings who usurped her role as the baby. She particularly resented having to forego her dreams of following in the professional footsteps of her only "lady teacher," all such hopes destroyed by the move to "America."

The Johana whom Martin returned to the last time must have been near the end of her tether. She was 41 when the twins were born and reputedly had suffered "complications." She kept Lillie home from school part-time to help look after the three younger ones and clearly relied on Martha and Sina for help as well. At meals, the three older girls were staggered around the table, each assigned the feeding of a much younger sibling. Martha left for Skudneshavn to get a job rather than take higher education. Johana arranged a scholarship for Sina, who dropped out in mid-year. Resentful at being asked to step in part way through so as not to lose the money, education-starved Lillie angrily refused to take Sina's place. Into the midst of what looks like a mother beginning to lose control over increasingly independent daughters, once again sailed Martin. The decision to leave for America curiously allowed parental authority to be re-established. The farm and equipment were sold, the girls were called home from their jobs, a deal was struck with Johana's sister Martha Wyberg in Bellingham to pay for young Martha's ticket in return for a period of free labor when she arrived, neighbors came to bid farewell and the family sailed into history as emigration statistics.

It must have been a very hard decision for Johana to make. When she arrived home from America nearly a quarter century before, she reportedly vowed never to leave Norway again. Now she was leaving, surely with no hope of returning. Undoubtedly, she underestimated just how badly this second try would turn out for her. Instead of having an honored position as district midwife, she would deliver babies for barter, her credentials rejected by Canadian authorities. Instead of a cosy bungalow and orchard, she would live first in a home dug into the side of a hill, then one constructed out of the same earth. In place of her dreams for her children, she would see them grow tough from hard work. Whatever personal dreams she might have had of founding a new dynasty in a new world, they could never live up to the honor she felt due the heritage and family she left behind.[28] Johana died within seven years of arriving in Alberta, predeceased by her daughter Sina, the family favorite. She handed the torch of family honor on to Ellenor, a woman with a fierce attachment to land, to history and to a sense of family importance.

Perhaps Johana truly believed the New World had changed significantly from the one she had fled two decades before. Perhaps she truly believed that Martin had planned this all well and would not plunge his family into difficulties. Certainly others believed in the dream. More than fifty years later, Ellenor wrote:

> *When it became definitely known that we were going to Canada, my broth-ers and I were the envy of the whole school. The wonderful illusions we had of this country were beyond the imagination. This was Utopia, and my idea of that was to wear silk dresses and patent-leather slippers every day; to live in a fine house and not have to wash any dishes. We were also much impressed with the scenery in the pamphlets showing the Rockies and big cattle ranches. (51)*

It was one thing for Norwegian school children to believe this. It was quite another thing for Martin, who had spent sufficient time chas-ing the American dream to have overwhelming evidence of its elusive-ness. Unlike that of the rest of his family, his life would change little. Apparently a man of great charm and vitality, Martin could walk at least twenty miles a day and loved travelling so much he kept logs even of ordinary trips. Tellingly, he demonstrated his impatience at not travelling by pacing the floor for hours at a time. He is remembered by his descen-dants as "the old gent," sailor, story-teller, tap-dancer, concertina-player, knot-tier, tobacco-chewer, boxer, player of tricks, writer of rhymes, owner of a pearl-handled revolver, hater of farming. A few years after his wife died in 1917, Martin moved to Bellingham and married his sister-in-law, Nille, widow of his brother Faltin. There, finally out of steam, he opened a shoemaking shop in his home, practising a trade he probably learned from Skule Ola. He died 8 August 1939. His only surviving son, Martin, Jr., refused to go to his funeral.

A member of a manuscript review committee who reviewed an earlier draft of this introduction took umbrage with what she saw as my portrayal of Johana—and later on, Ellenor—as somehow victims of their husbands. I was tweaked for my seeming inability to understand that good wives support their husbands.[29] The interesting question of course is not whether this view of heterosexual marriage *holds* true but why it should be *held* to be true. Jill Ker Conway and others have in fact made the very point that the reason the study of gender is so fruitful is for what it tells us not about men and women but about social and cultural sys-tems. The idea that our array of choices for traditional marriage need be limited to victimizer/victim or supporter/supportee seems the child of an unusual poverty we need not accept as our scholarly lot.

My examination of Johana's and, later, Ellenor's motivations for fol-lowing their husbands into exile is in the spirit of honest enquiry. The answer, indeed, need not reflect favorably on either woman. Historians of professional women have pointed out that what have been called "superperformers" have sometimes felt impelled "to go to great lengths to avoid any intimation that they might be shirking their duty as mothers and wives."[31] Perhaps Johana, a woman who had certainly out-performed her husband, was motivated by a desire to prove to whoever was watching that she measured up, matrimonially and maternally speaking. And perhaps Ellenor in her own turn found in her own husband's needs an acceptable reason for her own failure to succeed at what she portrayed as her life's work. Patriarchal systems leave women bereft of neither choices nor explanations.

Other reviewers of this introduction have asked me to place more stress on the perils of pioneering for women. As Nanci Langford has pointed out in her 1994 doctoral dissertation, our knowledge of women's participation in the peopling of the prairies is "wanting."[32] Her work goes some distance in redressing this. Langford cites among her sources letters and memoirs (often fragmentary) thankfully preserved in archives. She can also point to sources made more available by scholars such as Susan Jackel, who has edited pioneer women's accounts of their lives,[33] and Eliane Leslau Silverman whose *Last Best West*, based on extensive interview work, has just been re-issued.[34] In addition, there are a number of published memoirs, now generally out of print.[35]

Secondary sources such as the essays in *Standing on New Ground*[36] and Frances Swyripa's work on Ukrainian-Canadian women have also appeared recently.[37] Certainly none of this scholarship portrays the decision to enter pioneer life as one that a woman would take lightly. Although our scholarship on dower rights indicates that women certainly did not always understand the precariousness of their legal status in the new provinces,[38] we can hardly see the independent Johana as a woman who had no choice but to follow wherever Martin led her. She had managed to live pretty much without him for most of her married life. There is no indication that she could not have continued to do so, no matter what her values might have been. Able as she was to support both herself and her children, her decision to move to a new country must be regarded as free.

It is unlikely, however, that they were of precisely the same mind regarding their future. Martin probably sincerely believed in his own dreams of making it rich; Johana more likely just wanted to make a home—a better home—for herself and her children. This is not an unusual story in terms of settlement of the west. Wallace Stegner, grandson of Norwegian immigrants who prospered in Iowa, described his family's brief sojourn in Canada in *Wolf Willow*.[39] In an attempt to find meaning in his itinerant childhood, Stegner fictionalized his father in *The Big Rock Candy Mountain*[40] and was still pondering the situation not long before he died. "My father," he wrote, "was a boomer, a gambler, a rainbow-chaser, as footloose as a tumbleweed in a windstorm." It is the next sentence that turns adventure to tragedy: "My mother was always hopefully, hopelessly, trying to nest."[41] Laura Goodman Salverson, the child of Icelandic immigrants, was born in Winnipeg in 1890 and moved with her family to North Dakota, Minnesota and even Mississippi before they settled back in Winnipeg. Her parents buried two children in their wanderings; Laura did not start to learn English until she was eleven.[42] Another early settler, brought as a child to the same area the Olsens settled, left a short memoir aptly entitled "Restless Pioneers".[43]

Writing this experience through, then, was not an unusual approach to what can only have been a perplexing experience for a young child and Ellenor Merriken started to do so as she approached the age of sixty. She was still writing it through, revising and sometimes changing the story, the year before her death at almost 91 on 3 February 1990.

In addition to the memoir reprinted here, Ellenor self-published three other books. Only her novel *Beyond the Survey*,[44] is set once again in Alberta. It takes the form of a trilogy, set in Cold Lake, spanning the years 1900 to 1919. Another of the self-published books is *Herring Hill*,[45] a combined history and memoir set in Federalsburg, Maryland—hometown of Ellenor's husband, Roy, and her own home for the last 53 years of her life. The remaining piece of her writing that is between covers is *Pansy Opossum*,[46] an illustrated tale for young children. In addition, she left a rewrite of *The Nose Hills Country*, re-titled *Canada: Land of Promise* (100 pp.), a description of her husband's earlier pioneering efforts in Saskatchewan (41 pp.) and further material on the family's difficult re-establishment in Maryland (36 pp.) There are also a few newspaper clippings, verse and other loose pages. While all these sources provide biographical material and insight into Ellenor's approach to her life and to her work, none come near the quality of *The Nose Hills Country* in either literary or historical terms. There is about this book a freshness and engagement that make it alone worth republication. However, although I use the other works here only as back-up resources, it should be noted that they contain a wealth of detail and insight into pioneer life and the long-term effects it had on those who experienced it.[47]

The Nose Hills Country contains practically nothing on Ellenor's earlier life in Norway: we are in Alberta by the middle of the first chapter and on the road to a possible homestead by the end of it. When that venture fell through, the Olsens relocated to the country near the new settlement of Coronation. They lived in a one-room sidehill dugout until a sod house—a form of architecture they had glimpsed with horror from the train windows on their way across the prairies—could be built. By this point, a year had elapsed since landing in Canada. Johana brought out one of her best tablecloths, covered the hand-hewn table and decreed: "Children, let us be thankful. We are home at last." (66)

The early part of Ellenor's memoir is written very much from the child's point of view. Martha and Lillie left their family at Winnipeg in order to join their Aunt Martha in Bellingham, Washington and earn money first to pay back Martha's ticket and then to help their parents' establish a homestead they had never seen and would never own. Sina also took a job, as a waitress, in Castor, Alberta, the end of the rail at that time. She too sent money home. While all three girls visited and eventually settled near the homestead, Sina and Lillie opening their own restaurant in the new town of Veteran,[48] the three younger children grew up pretty much as a separate family.

Ellenor's engagement with the new country is palpable and her appreciation for community life visceral. The children worked hard but were also given free range of the prairie, inventing games often involving duped farm animals, learning to hunt and kill and befriend wild animals, playing mostly with one another, sometimes with other children. There is a sense of equality that crosses the child/adult line. Many of the inhabitants of the area were bachelors, desperate for family life. They came to eat Johana's meals, stayed to play with the children, taught them how to ride and shoot, lending them their horses and guns during the visit. The bachelors also seemed to be the driving force behind much of the social life of the community, arranging ball games, the famous Big Gap Stampede, track and field meets, the annual picnic. When it came time to build a school, one bachelor donated land and others agreed to pay their part of the taxes on the condition that the school also serve as a community hall for dances. Music was provided by anyone who could play an instrument.

Single women were in short supply in this environment and

Ellenor attended her first dance—in a bachelor's shack—at age 12. She danced every dance; the odds were 5 women to 9 men. When she was 13, an unsuitable suitor who wanted to marry any of the sisters and who was strung along as a joke by Martin, made a firm offer for Ellenor and was sent packing by Johana. A year later, Ellenor met Roy Merriken, new to the district from Saskatchewan, almost twice her age, a baseball star and someone who seems to have courted both Lillie and Sina as well. Perhaps Ellenor was competitive with her older sisters, eager to grow up, or perhaps she was simply genuinely attracted to this romantic older man, one whom she says all the girls were after.

Life was wearing for women in this new country. Roy's sweetheart back in Maryland married another rather than face the hardships he underplayed in his letters home to her, overplayed in his letters home to his mother.[49] Ellenor's manuscript is populated with doomed and endangered women: her own mother, her favorite sister, the neighbor who treated her as a daughter, a starving woman with a husband away looking for work, all dead; a woman dying after being taken in great pain to hospital, a woman surviving surgery only by a miracle; husbands riding through deep snow to find doctors to deliver babies, women in labor walking miles to a neighbor's so as not to deliver alone. Ellenor herself was the sole attendant at the birth of her sister Sina's first child. Martha's first confinement was attended instead by tragedy: the boy survived but his twin, a girl, was buried in a corner of the yard. It is ironic that this family, in getting its two sons away from the dangerous North Sea, landed its four daughters on the dangerous prairies. While she was alive, Johana gave of her own medical knowledge freely but there was no-one to look after her when she was sick and out of food, Martin away threshing, the younger children making pancakes for her with hawk's eggs rummaged for along the sloughs.

It called for a special type of woman not only to survive in this country but to embrace it as Ellenor did. And there were severe restrictions on just how she was allowed to embrace it. At one point, she took a job herding cattle and declared herself "a regular cowgirl." She loved it but went home when called to look after Martin and the twins, "who were tired of batching." (113) Like her sisters—who sent home money for clothing and shoes and machinery so that the rest of the family might remain on the homestead that the two boys would take over in turn— Ellenor's first duty was to male relations, not to herself. The only acceptable way to escape from this was to marry. It is of note that shortly after her marriage to Roy, her father and her brothers all married, each finding another woman to perform the necessaries.

The gender divisions of this culture are striking, all the more so because they are in some ways so blurred. Ellenor revelled in her own ranching and farming skills but was well-trained to obscure them in a society devoted to maintaining the patina of gender difference—where men are men and pay ten cents a dance to subsidize the evening's entertainment; where ladies are ladies and bring cakes. Cruel jokes and ostracism were used to maintain this order. Henry Davis, Roy's friend since childhood and partner for more than ten years before Roy's marriage, is ridiculed for his failure to make the house nice for the newlyweds on their return from their honeymoon. Another character, a successful local rancher who swings off her horse "in real cowboy" fashion and finishes off Johana's potato pancakes is labelled "queer." This woman's recognition of Ellenor as a kindred spirit is unwelcome to her, despite Ellenor's repeated references to her pride in her abilities to surpass her brothers. The scene is eerie:

> All of a sudden, she took one look at me, gulped and swallowed a couple of times and blurted out, "I'll bet you can ride like an Indian!" I almost fell backward, and began to look for some excuse to get away. Mama told her that I could ride as well as any boy, Indian or white. She was determined to take me home with her for a visit to help her round up her horses. I didn't know what Mama would say to that, so I sneaked outside and was not to be found. She came back several times and we never did find out what she really wanted, since her horses did not graze in our part of the country. She may have meant well enough but I had the most peculiar feeling about her, and whenever I saw her heading in our direction, I jumped on my pony and rode around until she was out of sight. (98-99)

Compare this to Ellenor's first meeting with Roy: she is wearing pants, skinning a team of oxen, working with the threshing team, hating "to display my skill in front of all those men." (103) Roy makes a joke first of her skill, then of her name. Embarrassed, she still finds this, for some reason, attractive. When next they meet, he again teases her about her name. When she rebuffs him, he seems hurt, compliments her thick auburn hair and tells her that "he wanted more than anything to learn to dance," would love to take her to the dance. (104) Since Ellenor's later manuscript on Roy's earlier life in Saskatchewan describes a triumphant evening where—after nightly lessons from his roommate—he outpolkas the fiddler, [50] we have to assume this is a come-on of some type.

Clearly, there was a dance going on here whose intricate steps had to do with something other than honest communication between two people looking for a partner in the business venture of pioneering.

The deciding point in the relationship came when, at age 19, Ellenor spent several months at business school in Calgary. Seizing the opportunity of her brief visit home before taking up a job in the city, Roy began to visit regularly, paying court. "It didn't take him long to convince me that I would make a better farmer's wife than secretary." (118) Ellenor's turn of phrase here is most interesting: choosing a career, not simply choosing a man. Given how embedded she was in the life of this community, the decision is understandable. Moving to Calgary meant uprooting herself once again; starting out as a secretary meant learning new skills, not honing the ones in which she already took considerable pride. Furthermore, there must have been echoes of the move from the old country and of the struggle the family had reestablishing itself, a struggle she knew had been disastrous for her mother, forced to shift from midwife to farmwife, from a family with an estate to a family in a sod house.

Just how hard psychologically it might have been for Ellenor to reestablish herself is made clear by the pain she later expressed at having to start over again in Maryland at the age of 38 in 1937. By the time she married Roy in Edmonton on 11 December 1920, he was already having to face the toll that age takes on childhood rheumatism. Although Ellenor, in response to his offer, chose the life of a farmer over that of a businesswoman, when Roy decided to move his family to his old home for his own health, she was forced to recreate her mother's life, struggling to start anew, opening and building up a feedstore. Determined and strong, Ellenor coped and thrived but she always stayed a stranger in a strange land, an expatriate from the big-sky prairie confined to a peninsula peopled with old-timers who greeted her as a foreigner. As her daughter, Jean, has said to me, "Mother never really left Alberta. It was always home to her."

The last third of *The Nose Hills Country* describes the first 17 years of Ellenor's and Roy's married life. She presents them and their growing family as eager participants in community social life, particularly in terms of sports events. Although the 1920s was a disaster for many settlers to the prairies,[51] Ellenor makes no mention of hard times. That decade slides by as a series of vignettes: acquisition of a model T car, ice cream parties, sports days, drunken male high jinks on hog shipping day, visits to and from Roy's folks, Lyal's paralysis overcome, incompetent slum labor from Britain taken in and fed, an arrogant cousin taken in from California and made a man of, picnics, berry-picking, the appearance of fences and roads, cooking for threshers, getting children schooled, attending Christmas concerts and parties, rounding up horses, carding wool, making quilts, playing cards, making rugs, building a church. The Merrikens do not seem to have been much involved with the political life of their community. One casual reference is to meetings of the newly established United Farmers of Alberta, the women retiring to the girls' cloakroom when they "felt like drifting off on some strictly feminine subject like cooking or sewing." (148)

For Ellenor, the Thirties were definitely dirtier: "Farming was getting to be a hit and miss affair."(150) Talk turns to dustbowls, Bennett buggies, scant harvests, barbwire telephones, beef rings, tornadoes, dried-out farmers and ranchers trekking north in search of rain. At last, done in by discouragement and pain, Roy returns from a trip to Maryland, eager to move his family "home." *The Nose Hills Country* ends with Roy and Ellenor and their three young children setting out in the November snow to catch the train from Veteran. "I am going away," she says to the Hills, alone on a rise behind her house, "not for always. I'll be back."(156)

There can be no doubt that Ellenor Merriken's look at the country she loved suffers from idealization. This takes form not so much in what she puts in as what she leaves out. Noticeable in particular is the absence of domestic strife, seemingly as nonexistent as sex. Merriken waits to "fictionalize" the less pleasant types of marital discourse in *Beyond the Survey*. While the struggles of women are ever present (no doubt focussed for her by the early loss of both her mother and her sister), she says little about the hardships suffered by men, other than the death of her brother Ole in 1927 from pneumonia and, at the end, Roy's increasing debility. Out all day in heat and cold, an out-of-proportion responsibility fixed upon them by a patriarchal legal and social system, doing physically demanding work, many of them virtually alone for their whole adult lives: it is hard to fathom what made many of them continue, easy to understand why Roy—who *could* go home, *did* go home. Again, this was for Ellenor a theme for fiction, not for "fact." In particular, the theme of male loneliness is explored in *Beyond the Survey*.

Also, in her sentimentality for community life, Merriken failed fully to consider the role of the outsider. In addition to Mamy Purtee, the woman whose honest admiration Ellenor finds more off-putting than

male teasing, there is a deaf-mute, called only Dummy by the other settlers, blamed (possibly justly) for setting a prairie fire. The only "Natives"
are Wild Indians played by masquerading cowhands dressed up for the
Wild West Show at the Big Gap Stampede and the buckskinned and
beaded entertainer who sings "Till We Meet Again" at the end of the
Chatauqua. Once more, *Beyond the Survey* takes up the topic, introduc-
ing a character Mowees (obviously an "Indianification" of the common
Metis name Moise) who unfortunately never rises above the level of a
Tonto figure.

Perhaps Ellenor's idealization of the Nose Hills Country would
have survived had she spent the rest of the Thirties there and an old age
of change and loss. Perhaps not. The move to Maryland was clearly trau-
matic for her. To her surprise and anger, Ellenor found that many of the
social skills acquired in the new communities in the shadow of the hills
were redundant and even inconvenient in a culture in many ways as
established and narrow as the one her father had found so unbearable in
Norway. Newcomers were not treated the way newcomers were treated
back home where every new settler was a much needed neighbor, a possibility of help in hard times, a statistic needed to justify government-
provided services such as schools and roads. Like her mother on Karmoy,
Ellenor had mattered in the Nose Hills. She could help people, she could
run things, she was somebody. Now, again like those of her mother, her
"credentials" were not recognized. Along this eastern, settled seaboard,
with established families and established services and established manners, she was an interloper assigned a long apprenticeship before she
could win acceptance.

Perhaps her apprenticeship was unintentionally, inevitably, extended by her own refusal to give up her prairie ghost. Only in old age did
she seem finally to accept the turn her life had taken before middle age.
Her later rewrite of *The Nose Hills Country* ends more poignantly, with
more finality. Written in her 80s, after the homestead (rented out for
decades with Martin, Jr.'s help, only a small shack kept to store some family possessions) had finally been sold, and after Roy had died, her new
ending tells of Roy sending her back after they are a little way down the
trail to retrieve the box that holds her auburn hair, cut off one hot summer afternoon without his permission. At last she is able to declare the
move "the end of an era for us."[52]

The fact that Ellenor Merriken rewrote in this fashion is evidence
that she saw herself as a writer, not simply as a keeper of a family chron-

icle. In addition, her decision to go to the trouble of getting her own writings printed up at her own expense, and in relatively large numbers, clearly indicates that she wanted to reach a wider audience; she wanted to be read. All the printed works are self-published and, in her 83rd year, she was looking for a way to distribute 1000 copies of *Beyond the Survey* in storage in Red Deer, Alberta.[53] The decision to try fiction is a further indication of serious professional commitment. However, although there exist clippings on her various activities in the Federalsburg newspapers, the only published recognition of her work has heretofore been the reproduction of short excerpts from *The Nose Hills Country* in a book of documents on Canadian women.[54]

What motivated her? It certainly could not have been money, since she started too late and had no access to profitable marketing of her work. Certainly, she had an investment in getting her version of things on the record—and in leaving certain other things emphatically off the record. But I think her greatest motivation was to teach and in particular to teach about that curious human experience called pioneering.

That Ellenor had a fundamentally didactic nature is clear from her approach to writing fiction, demonstrated in both the novel and the children's book. The novel, *Beyond the Survey*, is a goldmine of detail on how to build a poverty box; how to break horses; how to plough a field; how to build a boat, fish on ice, preserve the catch; how to set a trap, skin the prey, get the goods to market; how to organize a rodeo, a picnic, a barn-raising.[55] In her foreword, she states: "This book will help you relive the past, and let you find out for yourself what life was like Beyond the Survey." In the children's book, *Pansy Opossum*, she cannot resist the line, "You see, my mom has two pockets underneath her tummy, one on each side, where she can carry as many as six babies." What matters at that point in the story is neither opossum anatomy nor reproduction but the fact that Pansy falls out and is left early to make her own way in life. In conventional terms, this does not constitute "good writing."

But it would be hasty to dismiss Merriken's writings simply on the grounds that they do not live up to some ideal of good literature. She was not trying to live up to that ideal. Neither was she a rebel, consciously challenging literary conventions, an ambition that might also have gained her serious literary consideration. Rather, she was trying to tell a story in the way she had been told stories, and for the reasons she had been told stories. That she was conscious of the sort of energy this naive approach has is clear from a letter she sent to relatives in 1974, complaining about unwanted editing to *Beyond the Survey* performed by a well-meaning typist.

> *This morning I received a letter . . . together with thirty pages of my story "Beyond the Survey" revised and flattened out in suposedly perfect grammar, in her version, of it. I wrote right back immediately, perhaps a little to soon, and asked her not to change it in any way, as it was written not for gramatical perfection, but to depict life in the early days when rugged men were trying to help build a new nation. Most of them couldn't speak English even. I told her just to punctuate it, and not to touch sentence structure or grammar. I can't have her ruin it; I would sooner let it lie idle. . . You cannot imagine how insipid and flat she made it, without the things I tried so hard to impart. The rugged life, the genuine stamina of the people and their way of making the best of what was there. I was real upset to say the least; as she hasn't the least idea what I was trying to bring forth. She has already retyped thirty pages that she included, and that I'll keep and burn after a while. I don't think it needs any editing at all, perhaps punctuation might not be a bad idea, but the printer will usually correct that.* [56]

Given the number of errors in this paragraph, it is difficult not to have sympathy for both the typist and the printer. Still, the power of expression is apparent and Merriken makes it clear that that is what she is after. Perhaps the best comparison is to the type of vigor preserved in and presented to us by naive painting. Described as "nonce art," naive painting has been said to have "no past and no future, it captures 'now' and freezes it forever."[57] The naive painter has been described as "a tribe of one member," marked by a unique personal vision.[58] A good comparison for Merriken is Irene McCaugherty, of southern Alberta, whose watercolors and drawings deal with many of the same themes: social events, rodeos and hard work.[59] McCaugherty's work is, like all good naive art, childlike and direct.

Naive painters have for quite some time been subject to serious appreciation by art scholars; naive writing is only just beginning to receive the same consideration as a type of, rather than an error in, literature. Helen Buss has written critically about the importance in particular of Canadian women's writings of this ilk.[60] She advises us to read between the lines, to read the absences as well as the traces. Finding a way to import such literary techniques into the discipline of history will allow us both to broaden our base of research and to use more effectively sources long available. This is important not only in terms of women's history but in all areas where sources are rare or "suspect."

As history, works such as Merriken's could be dismissed as fundamentally flawed. This is so not because of any failings of style but because of what she sees as their greatest attribute, the "true" story they tell. Her foreword to *The Nose Hills Country* states: "This is the story of my life. It is true in every detail, as I remember it." The foreword to the revised—and sometimes factually as well emotionally different—version of the same events written a quarter century later again states: "This is a true story of frontier days on the prairie of Alberta as experienced by the author."[61] But what is Merriken's definition of truth? It would seem that it encompasses not telling lies but that is not betrayed by the holding back of certain "truths." One person I talked to who knew Merriken when she lived in the Nose Hills Country and who clearly had enjoyed reading the book described Merriken as "careful," saying that Merriken "skimmed over them parts," meaning rough and scandalous stories. This was okay, though, said the woman, because "anyone who knows the real story can figure out what's going on."[62] These are stories, then, not just about imparting information but about imparting it selectively and for a distinct purpose.

A phenomenon in Alberta over the past couple of decades has been the community history, a compilation of stories and photographs put together by a volunteer committee whose members solicit family histories and community anecdotes. The one relevant to the Nose Hills Country is *Where the Prairie Meets the Hills*.[63] While it serves as the major back-up check for Merriken's stories, it suffers from many of the same "flaws" as an historical resource. While all these histories make fascinating reading, it does not take long to find inconsistencies of spelling, punctuation and, well, fact. But their verve is unmistakable. They have the energy of pool hall reminiscences, quilting bee gossip, after-church reportage. And that is their heritage. All forms of communication model themselves on earlier forms; everyone has to learn to speak somehow.

Both Merriken's works and the community histories are stories told to those who already "know the real story" but they also impart the salient features of that story to a different set of intended readers: those who come after. In her foreword to *The Nose Hills Country*, Merriken says, "I would not trade my childhood for the soft existence that youth now takes for granted. I have the satisfaction of knowing that I have had a part in the making of a great country." This last sentence could be used as a motto for each and every one of the community histories I have read, were its last phrase not so American.

There are two remarkable things about this sentence. One is its underlying sentiment of one-up-manship: not only has "youth" not experienced this hard life, it can never do so, can never catch up. Life has changed and is now too "soft" to provide the challenge necessary for proof of character. This is a common cry of the old to the young: "you didn't have all those babies;" "you didn't go to war;" "I walked five miles through snow drifts to get to school." Its effect is to alienate although its aim is probably to seek inclusion, to say "Don't overlook me, I used to be somebody." In its least attractive form, it is an attempt to lay the dead hand of the past upon one's descendants.

The other remarkable thing is its belief that all the personal deprivation this sort of literature is full of was worth it because there was a joint venture going on, a venture called pioneering, one that would bring European civilization to the New World. The Canadian prairies are unique in that they contain many settlements established within living memory, though those memories are failing us fast. The community histories are a group attempt to record that memory; Ellenor R. Merriken attempted to do it on her own.

She needed a model. Had she been more educated, she might have consciously chosen, as did Laura Goodman Salverson, that of the Scandinavian saga.[64] As it is, Merriken falls naturally into that mold when she writes the novel: it is a long detailed narrative largely unconcerned with psychological or historical depth. A number of people are put through a number of trials and move on in their lives, by learning not only what to remember but what to forget. In three parts, it deals with three related but separate stories, that of a young Norwegian immigrant who comes to Cold Lake, Alberta, and who adjusts to loneliness; that of Swedish neighbors who establish a viable homestead; and finally that of their son who grows up on the land, goes to war and retires to the woods for a year to recover from shell shock. It is significant that part of the son's confidence is restored by Nature having "erased the gruesome memories."[65] This is not a story about critical thinking and change; it is a story about acceptance and endurance, the key attributes required for pioneering.

An outstanding part of *Beyond the Survey* is its demonstration of Merriken's belief in the curative nature of story-telling, curative in the sense that it lays out exactly the standard of conduct expected and encourages the hearer in the belief that achievement of that standard is within her grasp. Martha Johnson, the Swedish homesteader, takes under her wing a young English bride who has moved in nearby. It is clear that the woman's new husband was not candid with her in his courting letters. She is miserable, lonely, eventually pregnant and emotionally dependent on Martha. Martha feeds her, sends bread home with her, tells her she'll just have to buck up, all to no avail. What finally does the trick is a story that takes up twelve pages of text in which Martha tells Hazel about the troubles her own parents had homesteading in Kansas. This is followed by her own story of enduring three years of drought before relocating to Alberta. She tells the girl, "Life is what you make it, Hazel. I have always tried to make the best of whatever has to be. That way nothing seems so very bad."[66]

But if story is curative, it is also didactic. It is one thing to expect people to buck up, it is quite another not to tell them how to manage it. Merriken's accounts of her life in Alberta are full of people helping people and, more often than not, this help comes in the form of basic information. These settlers were the first ones looking to bring European culture to this country. While people knew what they wanted, they could not always count on the old methods—even those learned in the United States—to carry it off. New information had to be assembled.

Dissemination of this new information was accomplished largely through oral communication, explaining the amount of instructional detail Merriken considers it appropriate to write as dialogue in *Beyond the Survey*. But there existed written precedents as well. Settlers to the New World, whose success depended partly on convincing others to join them, had long sent home letters that emphasized the riches to be gained but that also contained a great deal of information. It is likely that Merriken was familiar with the Norwegian version of these, "America letters,"[67] and that familiarity helps account for the didacticism of her works. She consciously set out to tell people how to succeed. At the same time, she had a very good idea of how precarious success was.

Ellenor Merriken did not find lasting success as a Canadian pioneer, and perhaps this was another of her motivations for writing about it over and over. While both her brother Martin and her sister Martha would manage to establish themselves on the land, Ellenor would not be able to stick it out. Like her mother, she too followed her husband when the word to go was given. Although she managed to hold on to land in the Nose Hills Country until 1974, although she managed to make the area and its history a focus of her children's view of themselves, although she came "home" whenever she could manage, Ellenor Merriken would—like so many others—be forced to give up and move on. She got on with her life but she never got over the loss of her second home. This failure as a pioneer must have been devastating for her, given the emphasis she put on perseverance in that role as proof of greatness, a theme which shows up not only in her printed works but in the texts of the manuscripts she left behind. At the same time, the fact that she left early, getting out fairly unscathed, living out the worst part of the Thirties in another area of the world that absorbed her animosity, no doubt accounts for some of her ability to feel nostalgia rather than bitterness. Still, her fondness for the life is no different from that of other memoirists of the prairies. One such account ends with the line: "It is, for me at any rate, the *only real way of life*."[68] Another ends with:

> *It was full of fun and good times, and if there were spear-grasses as well as shooting-stars, all in all I can't think of anything better than to have been homesteaders' children on the prairie of southern Alberta in the year 1904.*[69]

In 1959, at age 60, Ellenor Merriken went back to Karmoy for the first time and had her photo taken in front of the house in which she was born and had spent her first ten years. This single gesture seems to have been sufficient to satisfy any nostalgia she nursed for Norway: she wrote virtually nothing about her life there. When she looked for her country, it was always back to the Nose Hills. What follows is the most polished account she left of her life at "home." Its style is typical of the episodic nature of many such accounts. As editor, I have made perhaps a dozen changes to the original text and then only when necessary for understanding or to correct obvious spelling errors. I have not been able to muster the confidence that Lathrop E. Roberts could in editing his mother's manuscript, *Of Us and Oxen*. He abridged and rearranged and added, calling on his own "still very vivid" memory of the homestead. But, he avers, "Nothing in this editing has affected the authenticity of the story. This is my mother's book."[70] Those who might want to check this out will find the original manuscript in the Glenbow Archives.

The major change I have made to Merriken's manuscript is in the title, something I have not undertaken lightly. My chief reason for doing so is that Merriken's title is misleading. Although she seems to have looked at it as being a "history" of the area she lived in, it is memoir plain and simple. The title she gave her rewrite of the same material—*Canada, Land of Promise*—is equally off the mark. I doubt that she would have welcomed my interference but I have at least tried to honor her fascination for the geographical when it comes to naming a manuscript.

The strength of *Looking for Country* lies in the vitality and percep-tiveness of the memoirist. Ellenor was a good "noticer" and her enthu-siasm for this rich life is infectious. Although she was clearly critical in the sense of being judgmental, she was not so in the literary sense of the word. This means that much of her material comes to us like a good amateur photograph—composed and focussed but neither staged nor re-jiggered in the dark room. It is of particular importance to us because of the extreme rarity of complete documents of this sort written by women who are not privileged and whose first language is not English. A recent exception to the English-only rule is the publication of the letters of a Danish governess who came to Saskatchewan to marry a farmer in 1925.[71]

Merriken's *The Nose Hills Country* and her other works that cannot be offered here provide excellent material for the historian, material that Ellenor struggled to make available and which could easily have been lost to us. From the cover of the collection, *A Harvest Yet to Reap: A History of Prairie Women*,[72] a young woman carrying a gun in one hand and the fixings for dinner she has just shot in the other looks directly into the eyes of the beholder. Seeing that picture and reading this man-uscript for the first time gave me the same feeling. I can best describe it as a combination of connection and completion. 🦌

NOTES

1. Ellenor Ranghild Merriken, *The Nose Hills Country* (Canada: by the author, 1960), Foreword.

2. Leola Nelson Bergmann, *Americans from Norway* (Philadelphia: J.B. Lippincott Company, 1950), p. 41. Although Bergmann is addressing specifically the emigration from Norway to the United States, the same point holds true.

3. The various sources from which these and other general statements are drawn are cited here in the notes on specific points of information.

4. Gulbrand Loken, *From Fjord to Frontier. A History of Norwegians in Canada* (Toronto: McClelland and Stewart, 1980), p. 6.

5. Theodore C. Blegen, *Norwegian Migration to America, 1825-1860* (New York: Arno Press, 1969), p. 5.

6. Members of a movement for the revival of devoutness in the Lutheran church. There were 53 Sloopers when they landed after fourteen weeks at sea.

7. Odd S. Lovoll, *The Promise of America. A History of the Norwegian-American People* (Minneapolis: University of Minnesota Press, 1984), p. 8-11.

8. Ingrid Semmingsen, *Norway to America. A History of the Migration* (trans. by Einar Haugen; originally pub'd Oslo, 1975; Minneapolis: University of Minnesota Press, 1978), p. 120.

9. Lovoll, p. 29.

10. Semmingsen, p. 112-3.

11. Loken, p. 17-23. Norway House, established in what is now Manitoba in the early 1800s, was named for Norwegian axe-men who opened communications between there and York Factory. It was not a centre for Norwegian settlement.

12. By 1967, there were 42,000 residents of Norwegian background in Alberta, the largest in any province. See Jan Harold Brunwand, *Norwegian Settlers in Alberta* (Ottawa: National Museum of Man, 1974), p. 1.

13. Paul Voisey explores the various motivations for relocation of farmers in *Vulcan: The Making of a Prairie Community* (Toronto: University of Toronto Press, 1988), p. 33-5.

14. Carlton C. Qualey, *Norwegian Settlement in the United States* (Northfield, Minn.: Norwegian-American Historical Assn., 1938), p. 170.

15. Loken, p. 41. Loken has a section specifically on Norwegian settlement to Alberta on p. 55-76.

16. See Wendy Lee Karhoffer, "Visions of a New Land: Government Recruitment of Norwegian Immigrants to Alberta, 1870-1930" (Unpublished M.A. thesis, University of Calgary, 1991).

17. Lovoll, p. 8.

18. Howard Palmer and Tamara Palmer, *Alberta. A New History* (Edmonton: Hurtig Publishers, 1990), p. 71. Camrose would remain the centre for Norwegian culture in Alberta. Augustana University, formerly Camrose Lutheran College, served as a mainstay of that culture. Some of its original minutes are in Norwegian. See Charles A. Ronning, "A Study of an Alberta Protestant Private School: The Camrose Lutheran College, a resident high school" (Unpublished M.A. thesis, University of Alberta, 1943).

19. Daisy Lucas, "A Pioneer Norwegian Family," *Alberta History* 41 (no. 4, Autumn 1993) 16-19.

20. See Muriel Eskrick. *The Norwegian Settlers. Eagle Hill and Bergen* (n.p.: n.p., 1971).

21. Audiotape, Ellenor Merriken and Jean Merriken Andrew, Federalsburg, Maryland, 23 March 1988.

22. "Lillie Olsen's autobiography", New Westminster, B.C. (?), 1967 (?), manuscript, 39 pp.

23. Quoted from Chester Ronning, *A Memoir of China in Revolution* (New York: Random House, 1974), p. 5. Loken, p. 36.

24. 24 June and 17 May, respectively.

25. Geneological data comes from "Our Norwegian Family Tree", compiled by Lyal N. Merriken, Ellenor's son, in 1984. Family papers.

26. Material relating to Martin and Johana Olsen is taken from Lillie's manuscript, from a manuscript entitled "Part of my Family History" (n.d., 7 pp.) by Ellenor and from interviews with family members.

27. Lillie Olsen's autobiography, p. 5.

28. Among other things, there exist family stories of a forebear who rescued blockaded cities from starvation and of a huge inheritance denied the family by the state.

29. Anonymous, University of Toronto Press, November 1997. Although I have made no enquiries as to the identity of the reader in question, I assume it to be female for the simple reason that it is unlikely a man would have gotten away with such an unexamined view of the proper role of women.

30. Introduction by Jill Ker Conway, Susan C. Bourque and Joan W. Scott, eds., *Learning about Women. Gender, Politics, and Power* (Ann Arbor, Mich.: The University of Michigan Press, 1989), xxxix.

31. Miriam Slater and Penina Migdal Glazer, "Prescription for Professional Survival," ibid., p. 121.

32. Nanci L. Langford, "First Generation and Lasting Impressions: The Gendered Identities of Prairie Homestead Women" (unpublished Ph.D. dissertation, University of Alberta, 1994), p. 7.

33. Georgina Binnie-Clark, *Wheat and Woman* (Toronto: University of Toronto Press, 1979; originally 1914) and *A Flannel Shirt & Liberty: British Emigrant Gentlewomen in the Canadian West* (Vancouver: UBC Press, 1982).

34. Eliane Leslau Silverman, *The Last Best West. Women on the Alberta Frontier, 1880-1931* (Montreal: Eden Press, 1984, revised and updated Calgary: Fifth House, 1998.)

35. There are numerous examples of these, many listed in Carol Fairbanks and Sara Brooks Sundberg, *Farm Women on the Prairie Frontier: A Sourcebook for Canada and the United States* (Metuchen, N.J.: Scarecrow Press, 1983). As a recently republished example, see Mary Hiemstra, *Gully Farm. A Story of Homesteading on the Canadian Prairies* (Calgary: Fifth House, 1997; 1st ed., Toronto: McClelland Stewart, 1955).

36. Catherine A. Cavanaugh and Randi R. Warne, *Standing on New Ground. Women in Alberta* (Edmonton: University of Alberta Press, 1993).

37. Frances Swyripa, *Wedded to the Cause. Ukrainian-Canadian Women and Ethnic Identity, 1891-1991* (Toronto: University of Toronto Press, 1993).

38. See Catherine Cavnaugh, "The Limitations of the Pioneering Partnership: The Alberta Campaign for Homestead Dower, 1909-25," *Canadian Historical Review*, LXXXIV (no. 2, June 1993). For an angry portrayal of the courtship, marriage and desertion of one Jenny but John Tightwad, see the cartoons and captions reprinted in Barbara E. Kelcey and Angela E. Davis, eds., *A Great Movement Underway: Women and The Grain Growers' Guide, 1908-1928* (Winnipeg: The Manitoba Record Society, 1997), 119-23. Women certainly were not backward about their sense of vulnerability by the time of publication in 1914.

39. Wallace Stegner, Wolf Willow. *A History, a Story and a Memory of the Last Plains Frontier* (1st edition, 1955; Toronto: Macmillan, 1977)

40. Wallace Stegner, *The Big Rock Candy Mountain* (Garden City, New York: Doubleday, 1973; originally published 1943).

41. Wallace Stegner, "Finding the Place: A Migrant Childhood", in *Where the Bluebird Sings to the Lemonade Springs. Living and Writing in the West* (New York: Random House, 1992), p. 3-21 at 3. Originally published in *Growing Up Western*, edited by Clares Backes (Knopf, 1989).

42. Laura Goodman Salverson. *Confessions of an Immigrant's Daughter* (Toronto: University of Toronto Press, 1981), p. 6-9.

43. Evelyn Slater McLeod, "Restless Pioneers," *The Beaver* 307 (no. 1, summer 1976) 34-41.

44. Ellenor R. Merriken, *Beyond the Survey* (Red Deer, Alberta: Pacific Coast Publishing, Ltd., 1979).

45. Ellenor R. Merriken, *Herring Hill: A Historical Biography of Local Interest* (Denton, Maryland: Baker Printing Co., 1969).

46. Ellenor R. Merriken, *Pansy Opossum* (n.p.: n.p., n.d.).

47. The materials are currently in my hands. I have approached the Glenbow Alberta Archives about accepting them.

48. Towns along the route of the railway being built from the west had a boom/bust

cycle which depended on their status as supply centres at the current "end of rail." At the time the cafe was opened, Veteran would have held that momentary advantage. By 1912, end of track lay to the east at Consort. Bessie Smith and Joyce Gould, eds., *The Sunny Side of the Neutrals. Stories of Consort and District in Alberta—Canada* (Consort: Association of Consort and District Seniors, 1983), p. 2.

49. Saskatchewan manuscript, n.d., p. 21.

50. ibid, p. 32.

51. David C. Jones, *Empire of Dust. Settling and Abandoning the Prairie Dry Belt* (Edmonton: University of Alberta Press, 1987).

52. Ellenor R. Merriken, "Canada. Land of Promise", p. 100.

53. Letter, Ellenor R. Merriken, Federalsburg, Maryland to Beth Light, Ontario Institute for Studies in Education, 17 August 1982.

54. Beth Light and Joy Parr, eds., *Canadian Women on the Move, 1867-1920* (Toronto: New Hogtown Press and OISE, 1983), 74-75. The excerpts are from pp. 6-7, 27 and 85 of *The Nose Hills Country*. I had discovered a copy of the book in the Glenbow Archives in 1974 and brought it to the attention of the editors.

55. There exists another naive Norwegian-Alberta novel written about the same time period. While it follows more carefully conventions of plot and dialogue, it is far less useful as an historical document. Magda Hendrickson, *This Land is Our Land* (Calgary: Foothills Lutheran Press, 1972).

56. Letter, Ellenor R. Merriken, Federalsburg, Maryland to Ken and Hattie Olsen, Medicine Hat, Alberta, 24 September 1974. Merriken indeed may not have found conventional English forms entirely suited to her purposes. See Einar Haugen, *The Norwegian Language in America. A Study in Bilingual Behavior*, 2 vols. (Bloomington: Indiana University Press, 1969).

57. David Larkin, ed., *Innocent Art* (London: PanBooks, 1974), introduction.

58. George Melly, *A Tribe of One. Great Naive Painters of the British Isles* (Oxford: Oxford Illustrated Press, 1981), p. 7.

59. See Joan Stebbins, Catalogue, Irene McCaugherty Exhibition (Lethbridge: Southern Alberta Art Gallery, 1982).

60. See Helen M. Buss, *Mapping Our Selves. Canadian Women's Autobiography in English* (Montreal and Kingston: McGill-Queens Press, 1993). Also "Women and the Garrison Mentality: Pioneer Women Autobiographies and their Relation to the Land" in *Rediscovering our Foremothers. Nineteenth-Century Canadian Women Writers*, edited by Lorraine McMullen (Ottawa: University of Ottawa Press, 1990). For an example of American scholarship, see Brigitte Georgi-Findlay, *The Frontiers of Women's Writing. Women's Narratives and the Rhetoric of Westward Expansion* (Tucson: The University of Arizona Press, 1996).

61. "Canada. The Land of Promise", 1986.

62. Interview, name withheld, Veteran, Alberta, 1 August 1995.

63. Elba and Angus Anderson and Shirley Vetter, editors, *Where the Prairie Meets the Hills. Veteran, Loyalist and Hemaruka Districts* (Calgary: Friesen Printers, 1977).

64. See Rosaleen McFadden, "Icelandic Edda and Saga in Two Prairie Novels: An Analysis of *The Viking Heart* by Laura Goodman Salverson and *Wild Geese* by Martha Ostenso" (Unpublished M.A. thesis, Concordia, 1971).

65. *Beyond the Survey*, p. 201.

66. ibid., p. 97.

67. For examples and discussion of America letters, see Peter A. Munch, *The Strange American Way* (Carbondale and Edwardsville: Southern Illinois University Press, 1970) and Carlton C. Qualey, trans. and ed., "Seven America Letters to Valdres" in *Norwegian-American Studies*, vol. 22 (Northfield, Minnesota: Norwegian-American Historical Association, 1965), p. 144-61.

68. Kathleen Strange, *With the Wind in Her eyes. The Story of a Modern Pioneer* (Toronto: George J. McLeod, 1937), p. 292.

69. Georgina H. Thomson, *Crocus and Meadowlark Country. A Story of an Alberta Family or Recollections of a happy childhood and youth on a homestead in southern Alberta* (Edmonton: the Institute of Applied Art, 1963), p. 277.

70. Sarah Ellen Roberts, *Of Us and Oxen* (Saskatoon: Modern Press, 1968), foreword.

71. Craig W. Miller, ed., *Union of Opposites. Letters from Rit Svane Wengel* (Regina: Canadian Plains Research Center, 1996). For a discourse on the problems and rewards of doing ethnic history, see Franca Iacovetta, "The Writing of English Canadian Immigrant History," The Canadian Historical Association, Canada's Ethnic Group Series, Booklet no. 22. (Ottawa: CHA, 1997).

72. Linda Rasmussen, Lorna Rasmussen, Candace Savage and Anne Wheeler, *A Harvest Yet to Reap. A History of Prairie Women* (Toronto: Women's Press, 1976).

Family gathering, ca. 1920s.

*Johana Olsen
with Sina and
Martha (standing),
ca.1892.*

*Below: Olsen home, Island of
Karmoy, Norway.*

Johana, Martha, Martin Jr., and dog Jip in front of Olsen sod house, near Veteran, Alberta, 1912.

"Going places," Martin Olsen, Sr.

Lillie Olsen on Goose Lake, ca.1915.

Martin Jr. and Ole, ca.1916.

*Martin Olsen Sr., in Bellingham,
Washington, ca.1920s.*

Roy Merriken, Coronation, Alberta, 1913.

Ranghild Olsen, 1915.

Wedding photo of LeRoy S. Merriken and Ranghild (Ellenor) Olsen, December 11, 1920.

Merriken homestead, near Veteran, Alberta, ca. 1930s.

Threshing at the Nose Hills. The Merriken homestead looked out onto these hills.

"Cowboy Roy," ca.1919.

*Lillie and Ellenor
(Ranghild), ca.1925.*

*Ellenor (Ranghild) at
Catalina, California,
1927.*

Lyal and Marie Merriken riding to school, 1930.

Roy Merriken and Johnny Johnson at cabin at Cold Lake, Alberta - site of "Beyond the Survey," 1935.

Ellenor (Ranghild) with daughters Marie (left) and Jean.

Ellenor (Ranghild) (seated) and Lillie, 1950.

Looking for Country
Ellenor Ranghild Merriken

Foreword

This is the story of my life. It is true in every detail, as I remember it. Names are real, places and incidents authentic. It begins with a child's reaction to leaving her homeland for a strange country, continuing through the experiences encountered by an immigrant pioneer family in the early days in Alberta and how they managed to cope with situations almost beyond belief. In spite of years of struggle and privation, I would not trade my childhood experience for the soft existence that youth now takes for granted. I have the satisfaction of knowing that I have had a part in the making of a great country.

Ellenor Ranghild Merriken,
Federalsburg, Maryland
1960

To the early settlers who endured hardship
to develop the Nose Hills Country,
this book is dedicated.

Chapter I

I T WAS ON THE ISLAND OF KARMOY OFF THE ROCKY COAST of Norway that I first saw the light of day. There were already three girls in the family, so naturally my parents expected and hoped for a boy, a son and heir to carry on the family name and traditions. My being a girl upset all their plans. I was to have been named after my maternal grandfather, Rasmus Hemnes. They rearranged it to Ranghild, a name I seldom use. Wanting a boy so much must have had an influence on my makeup, for I turned out to be a real tomboy. I have always enjoyed participating in boys' activities more than girls' and often could equal or beat the boys at their own games.

The very first thing that I remember was a long lonesome day when I could not see my mother. When they finally took me to her, I found two little red-faced babies in my cradle. These, my sister Sina told me, were brand new little twin brothers. There was much joy and celebration at the arrival of boys in the family at last, and two of them at one time! They were named Martin and Ole. I was not quite two years old at this time and it was hard for me to understand why I had to be a big girl all at once, and I did resent having to relinquish my mother to these new babies. To pacify me, she promised that when the boys grew up, I would then get to be a baby again. Whenever she rocked them, I insisted on being there too but I had to stand up behind her and be the Captain. One day, when I was about three years old, it dawned on me that I had waited long enough, so I marched in front of her, stamped my little foot real hard and said, "I am tired of being big, I want to be little again."

The recollections of my childhood in Norway are pleasant ones. I started to school when I was five. I could read out of my book the very first day I went. My teacher was very much impressed until he looked and saw that I was holding it upside down.

Christmas is the most outstanding thing in my memory, the lovely Christmas tree loaded with pretty things and goodies that greeted us on Christmas morning and all the children of the neighbourhood who came in to admire it and get a treat. It was the custom to gather in a circle, holding each other by the hand while marching around the tree and singing our favorite carols, after which we were allowed to pick something off the tree, either an orange, candy, or cookie. Santa was kept busy replenishing the good things, as there seemed to be a never-ending supply and more and more little friends came by to wish us *glade jul.*

We lived on a small farm which was close enough to the ocean for the salty spray to cover our windows with specks at times of high winds. Every man was a fisherman; all depended on the sea for their livelihood and my Dad was no exception. He would ship out on a freighter and be gone a year at a time. There was always anxiety about his safety and whereabouts if it was time for his return and he was late getting in. After such a trip, he would then stay home for a year or two and fish on his own around the Island. The waters around there are among the most treacherous in the world and every man has to be a good sailor to survive.

He owned a fishing boat in partnership with one of our neighbors, who was his best friend. They fished together for years, then one day the partner took the boat out by himself. A storm blew up and he came up missing. From then on, we heard more and more about America and its advantages.

The sea hovered like a shadow of death over us; whenever a storm blew in from the Northwest, the inhabitants of the Island felt uneasy. The call of ships in distress was heard often. The menfolk kept vigil at times like these, all night long, to lend any assistance they could, swinging lanterns and warning ships that came too close to the rocks, in the sailor's code of the most dangerous places. There were also beachcombers on the alert and it was at the first sign of a few planks or a barrel of something tossed in by the waves that we knew another ship had crashed on the rocks and brave men had paid with their lives. It was after a night like this that Papa came home exhausted and I heard him tell my Mother, "It is not worth it, this forever battling with the sea. The toll is too great. I fear for the safety of our boys." It was his fear that prompted my parents to leave the security of their old home and go forward to seek a safer place for us, and start anew in a land far from the sea.

Descriptive literature began to pour in from overseas and it was quite a problem to decide where to go and which country held the best opportunity for making a living, Australia or Canada. Both countries needed settlers and described in glowing terms and inspiring language the wonderful prospects in store for energetic families. My Dad finally decided by tossing a coin. Canada won and from then on we kids were eager to get started.

We had two uncles in Alberta and they encouraged us to come there. They even promised to help us get settled. They knew of a farm we could move to, fully equipped with horses, machinery, cows and chickens. All the owner asked was to be able to make a home with us and live as one of the family. When it became definitely known that we were going to Canada, my brothers and I were the envy of the whole school. The wonderful illusions we had of this country were beyond the imagination. This was Utopia and my idea of that was to wear silk dresses and patent-leather slippers every day, to live in a fine house and not have to wash any dishes. We were also much impressed with the scenery in the pamphlets showing the Rockies and big cattle ranches.

It was a cool misty day in April 1910 that we boarded the little steamboat *Rogaland* at Skudesneshavn, bound for Stavanger, our first stop. A crowd had gathered to see us off and wish us *lukka paa reisen*. We had a lot of relatives and friends and there was much handshaking and well-wishing and tears. We all felt sad at leaving each other. The coast of Norway lived up to its reputation for rough sea that day. As soon as the boat left the dock, the Captain ordered all hands below deck and every hatch and porthole closed. Soon, we began to toss on the waves like a rubber ball and before long most of the passengers were sick. This first leg of our journey lasted two hours and it was with mixed emotions that we looked forward to our long sea voyage.

Stavanger was a lovely city even then. We went to the museum and railroad station; there I saw my first train. It was a real thrill to stand on the platform and watch the incoming locomotive thunder by.

We left Stavanger on a large ship bound for England. The North Sea was quite rough but nothing like the Norwegian coast. We spent most of our time on deck and watched until all we could see of Norway was a speck on the horizon. When it faded out of sight, I felt a lump in my throat and I could not hold back a couple of tears that trickled down my cheeks. Looking up, I saw I was not the only one. We landed in Newcastle the next day and boarded a train for Liverpool. The English countryside was beautiful and left quite an impression on all of us.

When we left England, we were aboard the White Star Liner, *Lake Champlain*. As we steamed out of the harbor, someone drew our attention to a giant liner at anchor and said it was called the *Titanic*.

The *Lake Champlain* was a steady ship but very slow. It took us twelve days to cross the Atlantic. The weather was fine and the sea calm. We encountered several icebergs off Newfoundland, and had to drift slowly until we were out of the danger zone.

We three little kids had a lot of fun on board. We explored the ship from one end to the other. One time we really got lost when we happened to venture down into the hold and saw where the fourth class passengers were kept. They slept in bunks all along the wall; they looked pitiful, swarthy and filthy. A waiter happened by with a dishpan full of salt herring; they closed in on him and each started to grab a fish apiece. The waiter just backed up a few steps and threw the whole panful right over their heads. A real fish scramble followed and the lucky ones came up grinning and pleased with their catch. About that time, our Dad had appeared on the scene, having been looking for us for nearly an hour. We promised never to wander off again if he would not tell our Mother where we had been.

My first glimpse of the New World came as we steamed up the St. Lawrence River toward Quebec. We stood with our eyes focused on the land. Our sea journey had been quite lengthy and since we had explored every foot of the ship, we were ready for new adventures. Canada welcomed all immigrants, without any strings or red tape. There was no such thing as assistance or relief either. Everyone paid his own fare and made his own living such as he could. The immigrant train stood ready to take its quota of settlers on westward and we were ushered aboard with a lot of others. My Dad could speak very good English and he acted as interpreter for those that could not; consequently, we were about the last ones aboard. It was here in the railway station in Quebec that I first tasted ice cream. The wonder of that discovery will stay with me always.

I have often wondered how my parents felt as they stood on the edge of a new world with everything they had known and loved left behind and only the spirit to go forward and carve a better civilization from the frontiers and wilderness and bring what wisdom and culture they possessed to soften the hardships they must have known they would encounter.

Our trip across Canada to Winnipeg was uneventful. Here two sisters, Lillie and Martha, separated from us and went on to Bellingham, Washington, to stay with our relatives there until we got settled. My three sisters, Lillie, Martha and Sina, were grownup young ladies by now. We three younger ones were like another set for we came late in our parents' life; they were forty years old when I was born; forty-two when the twins came along.

As we rolled on westward, we were fascinated by the endless prairie and herds of grazing cattle and horses and the occasional little black homesteader's shack. We began to get a little worried about the many little sod houses as the days went by. It looked as though this was the customary architecture of the prairie and a suspicion of what might be in store for us loomed in our minds. We brushed the thought aside, for had not Uncles Knud and Sivert written us many times, assuring us of that fully-equipped farm which we could move into?

The accommodation on this train was far from the luxury streamliners of today. The seats were hard wooden ones that could be made into a bed at night. We had to furnish our own bedding and cook our own meals on the old coal stove in one end of the car. Incidentally, this stove was the only heat in the car, too. We were fortunate to be seated in the end next to the stove. Those passengers at the other end of the car would crowd around the stove at night to keep warm. We were tired and worn out when we reached our destination, at the end of the sixth day of travel. It was ten o'clock at night when the conductor called out "Bawlf, next."

We all straightened up in our seats. The boys and I had been fully dressed for the last half hour. We had a tremendous amount of luggage and we were hoping someone would be there to meet us. Uncle Knud had sent his team and lumber wagon, with our cousin Jacob whom we had known in Norway, to meet us. It was good to see someone we knew and could talk to; he told us to call him Jack from now on.

We had never seen a lumber wagon before and this one had a triple box as well as three seats. As soon as the luggage was loaded, we kids climbed over the wheels and settled ourselves on the back seat. The difficulty arose when it came time for Mama to get in. They had to get a ladder before she could make it. Sina sat up front with Jack, and Papa and Mama in the middle seat. It was twelve miles on a muddy road to the farm. The moon was full and the air crisp, so we wrapped blankets around us to keep warm. The road was slippery, too, and there were signs of snowdrifts along the road. Jack let the horses walk all the way but long before we reached our destination, the three of us kids had slid off the seat onto the bags of featherbeds in the bottom of the wagon and were having pleasant dreams until Papa was shaking me gently, telling me to wake up and climb down.

Uncle Knud was a widower with five children: Olga, the oldest, was thirteen; Kristian was ten; Lars was eight; Anna was six and Louise was three. Olga was waiting up for us and had supper ready to put on the table. The lovely three layer cake in the centre of the table was a special treat that I'll always remember.

The next morning, we met our new cousins. They were a fine-looking bunch. They could all understand Norwegian but did not like to speak it. Finally they got tired of translating what they said all the time and talked Norwegian every time they were sure no one was listening. We started to school in a couple of days and were again the object of curiosity, for we couldn't speak a word of English. This was a small, one room country school by the name of Likness. There were several vacant seats and after all the other children were seated, we took those that were left. There happened to be a third grade reader in my desk, so I entertained myself by looking at the pictures as the teacher, having eleven grades in one room, did not have much time for foolishness. She finally got around to hear my reading lesson. She asked me something and when I did not answer, she up and hit me on the head. Kids can be very cruel too and we were made fun of and blamed for things we did not do, since we could not talk back to defend ourselves. This made us three stick close together and stand apart from the rest. We learned very fast, though, and before long we were able to understand a lot of what was said; it took longer to learn to express ourselves.

Our farm renting proposition fell through and we had to find some place to move to temporarily. There happened to be an old Log House on my uncle's place, which had been abandoned for some years. This seemed to be the only available place, so we moved in. With eight kids bunched up together, it had proved too much for both my Mother and Uncle, so it was agreeable to all that we separate. We planted a garden and a neighbor bachelor gave me a kitten. How happy I was to have something of my own that could understand me.

Our garden grew fine. We worked and weeded every day. It needed moisture and we soon got a soaking rain but we had not taken into consideration the roof of this house, which was sod, and the rain soon began to leak through. We mustered every kettle, pot and pan to catch the water that began to drip down on us. We had to put our bedding under the table. Fortunately, the table was a huge homemade one and there was lots of room under it. We had three umbrellas, so we kids got one each and sat under them until the rain stopped. Then one day my Dad brought home a cow, which we named Guro. She was an excellent milker, so we now had all the milk, butter and cream we could use and some to give away. I wanted so much to learn how to milk her and I did but wished many times afterwards that I had not been so anxious.

My parents tried hard to find a farm to rent or some place with decent buildings, without success. There were still homesteads to be had in several different parts of the province, so my Dad decided to find out something about it. He tried to borrow a saddlehorse but couldn't so he set out afoot, heading east. After a couple of weeks walking he was lucky enough to come in contact with an old friend, whom he had once known in Norway. This friend told him how to go about filing on a homestead and helped him to locate a quarter section of land close to his own farm. The only obstacle was that the land was open for cancellation instead of filing proper but they felt sure that he would get it and Dad came back in high spirits over the prospect of having a homestead of our own.

Next came the problem of transportation. Oxen—that was the answer. We could buy a team for one hundred dollars and a wagon for fifty dollars. Our neighbor, Mr. Brown, had a large herd of cattle, so Papa bought two three-year-old steers for fifty dollars each. They were as wild as steers can get, not having had a rope on them since they were branded. It took Mr. Brown and all hands, with the aid of a good saddlehorse, to rope and tie each one to a snubbing post and put rings in their noses. We couldn't begin to handle them without nose rings. We already had bought a wagon and a new set of harness. The ox harness is very simple as compared to the harness used on a horse. For an ox, it consists of a large leather collar with tugs and belly band and a rope for lines with snaps at the end to fasten in the nose ring to guide it. There is also a wide leather strap around the neck with a huge rolling snap that snaps into the ring of the neck yoke and holds up the wagon tongue.

The next thing was to get the oxen broken to work and another neighbor offered to do this for a certain small amount. He had a tremendous big ox that he used to break the young ones with and he promised to be back in the morning to start. The speed of an ox is no more than three miles an hour at best; this we did not know at the time. We waited until noon and had just about given up when he rolled in. Our steers were still tied to their posts. Papa had fed and watered them; they were so wild and mean we did not dare turn them loose.

We kids were really excited at the new adventure about to take place. The man was a real expert with oxen. We soon found out that he was equally proficient with profanity and, in spite of pleadings to stay and watch, we had to miss the performance and go to the house. He hitched first one, then the other steer with his own to the wagon and just before sunset he brought our two wild steers home, hitched together to the wagon, their tongues hanging out, eyes snapping and tails switching. Occasionally they would bellow, as if in protest. Their first lesson had been a good one. In years to come, Tom and Dick proved to be faithful and trusty and at times our very existence depended upon them. Papa had sailed the seven seas; worked in gold mines and lumber camps. About the only thing he knew nothing about was farming and I have often wondered why he chose to settle on the prairie.

On July 10, 1910, we were ready to hit the trail. Tom and Dick were becoming a bit more manageable every day. At first we had to use two ropes to lead them to water, one on each side, to keep them from charging us. Dick became tame much sooner than Tom and Papa could handle him by himself now. We had a real prairie schooner. Green willow twigs bent over the wagon box served as the framework for the canvas cover, with flaps at each end which we could snap shut in case it rained or pin back during the heat of the day. There, on the tail end gate, perched a chicken coop with six hens and a rooster. The cow was tied to the bolster by a rope around her horns. All our earthly belongings were stowed in the bottom of the wagon and levelled off to make a foundation for the six feather beds we had to sleep on; we three kids with our heads to the back and my parents with theirs toward the front of the wagon. I had reserved a place for my kitten too but misfortune befell her the day before we left, when Watch and Flory, Uncle's coyote hounds, came over and mistook her for a rabbit!

The sun was just peeping over the horizon as we started rolling along. Guro, the cow, stuck her feet in the ground and skidded along for a bit, not liking to be hauled around by the head. She soon realized that it was useless and fell in step. Pete, the rooster, crowed at intervals, which was very amusing to us kids. Our bed was made up and we were supposed to be sleeping, or at least resting, but the excitement was too great. We were so happy to be on our way.

One of the happiest memories of my childhood is of this trip. Every morning about peep of dawn, I would wake up and find that we were leisurely rolling along. With the flaps of the canvas pinned back, I could see my parents sitting on the wagon seat, their silhouettes against the sunrise and the soft glow that seemed to steal its way into our covered wagon mingled with the scent of wild roses, silver willows and grasses, sparkling with the early morning dew. This made an impression on my child's mind that I shall always remember.

Every morning at eight o'clock, we stopped to eat breakfast. This consisted of bacon and eggs, toast, jam and coffee, cooked over a camp fire. The cow had to be milked at this time, too. We would drink what we wanted, then pour out the rest. We had a constant supply with us and the only way to keep it fresh was to have it on tap. We hit the trail again at nine and drove until noon. We then let the oxen rest most of the afternoon. It was during this period that the heelflies were the worst. If these flies bit the oxen while we were on the road, they would make for the first brush patch or run right into a slough of water—wagon and all—and just stand there and switch their tails; nothing or nobody could persuade them to move.

Our final hitch for the day was from 4:30 to 8:00; we then made camp for the night. One of our chores was to exercise the chickens. We put a twine string on their legs before turning them loose. The rooster had to be tied to a stake, since he was more suspicious of us. We could catch the hens anywhere by stepping on the twine. Soon they got so tame that we didn't have to bother with the twine and could catch them anyway. They kept us in fresh eggs and it was a regular game we played to see which one of us found the most eggs.

We had no brake on the wagon, no breeching on the ox harness. This made it almost impossible for the oxen to hold back the loaded wagon when going down a steep hill. We kids soon learned to roughlock; this is to fasten a chain around the centre of the front axle and through the spokes of one hind wheel so that the chains pull under the wheel when it tightens. This made the wheel drag and works very well as a brake. As soon as we came to the bottom of the hill we had to undo the chain and get ready with chucks to put behind the wheels, going up hill. Every so often the oxen would have to stop and rest and get their wind again. When Papa would yell "chuck," we hurried to wedge the short piece of plank that two of us carried under each hind wheel of the wagon. Martin was handiest with the chain and Ole and I carried the chucks.

We were mighty glad when we reached Stettler. From there on it was level prairie and we had no need for brakes until we hit the coulees on Ribstone Creek. Here we had to ford through the mud and water to get across. We thought for a while that we would never make it. We had to stop and rest the oxen before attempting to climb the long hills and get on the level again. Shortly after we left Castor we spied a blue haze on the horizon. "That" Papa said, "is where we are headed for. Those are the Nose Hills." From that moment on my eyes were glued to that spot and as we drew nearer and nearer their outline became visible and I felt a secret fascination for them. Little did I realize that in the heart of those hills I was to spend the best part of my life.

Chapter II

We rolled into Vickres' place just at sunset on the sixteenth day. The oxen were getting sorefooted by now and the cow was tired. She had been pulling back on the rope the last few days, which made her head sore. We had to tie a white flour sack around her horns under the rope. I am sure we were a queer-looking outfit but that made no difference to the Vickre family. They met us with open arms. In all my life, I have never met anyone as kind and hospitable as Mrs. Vickre. She ushered us into the two room sod house, which was clean and homey, and as soon as we were comfortably seated, she put the big coffee pot on the stove. She had several different sizes and it all depended on the size of the crowd which coffee pot she would use. She was a marvellous cook and always had a variety of cake and cookies on hand. Five strangers did not seem to upset her routine a bit. We wanted to sleep in the wagon as we had been used to doing but they would not hear of it and instead gave us their own beds and slept on the floor, so we could have a good night's rest.

Our Homestead was one mile west of Vickres'. We were anxious to get to our own place, so we moved on over the next day and made camp. We had brought a tent along and a little camp stove. Papa was real handy with tools and before night he built a makeshift table. We had packed a lot of our stuff in wooden apple boxes and these came in handy to sit on. We made our bed on the floor of the tent. The animals were staked out on long chains down the coulee where the grass was good and there happened to be a spring of water, too. The chickens had to be put back into the coops to keep the coyotes from getting them. The mosquitoes were so bad that we had to build a smudge in front of the door of the tent, for they swarmed around us by the millions. In the daytime we wore mosquito nets on our hats and paper inside of long stockings. They couldn't seem to manage to bite through paper.

We dug a cellar and hauled logs for a house, as well as wood for the winter, from the Hills, but time seemed to creep up on us and soon Papa had to go back to Bawlf to harvest our vegetable crop. We had a letter from Uncle Knud saying that our garden had turned out wonderfully well. So Papa started out afoot, hoping that one of his brothers would bring him back with the load, since we needed the vegetables very much. The summer had been dry and hot; it was now the last of September. The nights were getting colder and we kept adding more bed clothes each night. Finally, one night a storm blew up and the next morning we found ourselves under a blanket of snow.

There happened to be a big sod house on a neighboring farm which was newly built and vacant, since the owner had gone away for the winter to find work. He had managed to get the outside walls up and the roof on but the inside was just one huge room with no ceiling and no partitions. This was far better than freezing in a tent and, besides, there was a lean-to barn attached to the house, for the animals. Since it was impossible for us to stay in the tent any longer, Mama decided to move into this place. She found out that it belonged to a young Swedish immigrant by the name of Emil Vallin and we took it for granted that he wouldn't object. In fact, he did not have the chance.

By this time we kids could handle the oxen quite well. Each of the boys had to stand and hold an ox by the nose ring to keep them from walking off after we got them hitched, while Mama and I loaded food, bedding and some wood. We managed to get into the sod house that night just before dark. As luck would have it, there happened to be an old tin heater-stove already set up and we huddled around that while the storm raged outside. We were waiting anxiously for Papa to come home. We had not heard from him since he left and wondered whether he would have to walk back or if he had been lucky enough to get someone to bring him and the precious vegetables. He didn't know that we had moved and we had no way of letting him know where we were. Then Mama happened to think about the lantern.

Back in Norway when he was out to sea, if it got dark before he made it to shore, she would light a lantern and set it on a certain cliff. He would always look for it and was guided safely home by it many times. She lit our lantern again and the boys climbed on the roof and fastened it to a pole that was up there for some reason. We waited for two days; the third night, he came. He said that he felt so strange when he first saw that light, for it was in the wrong direction, but something told him that Mama had put it there for him. He told Andrew to turn around and head for the light, and soon they were home.

We were overjoyed at seeing him safe and with a big load of stuff for us. Two young men with a team of horses and wagon were looking for homesteads and offered to bring his load home in return for help from him to locate a homestead for them. With two more in the family now this made it necessary for us to put up a partition in the big room. This is where the tent came in handy. We stretched it across the middle of the room, which gave us some much-needed privacy. Martin and Ole each got a puppy and I got a little black kitten that Papa found in a livery barn at Daysland.

Uncle Knud had let us have his Shorthorn bull, which made us have three oxen. We named this one King. Uncle Sivert had killed a pig and sent it along with all the potatoes, carrots, beets, cabbages and onions from our garden. We felt rich beyond measure and lucky to be alive. Papa got busy with hammer and saw and soon had a bed made out of poplar poles. With plenty of clean straw in the bottom, feather beds both under and on top of us and wool blankets between, it was soft and warm. It was a huge bed; all five of us had to sleep together to keep warm and quite often I tried to smuggle the kitten in, too. It was the only warm place we had and the reason for that was that it was occupied most of the time.

This was one of the coldest winters ever recorded. The thermometer hovered around fifty below zero for several weeks. A coat of frost half an inch thick had accumulated on the inside of the window panes. If we happened to hear sleigh bells near or a team drive by, we rushed to the window, scraped a hole through the frost, then blew on it until it was clear before we could see who was coming. In a matter of a few minutes, it would freeze over again. When Papa first got up in the morning, he would hurry to get his clothes on. This included his sheepskin coat, fur cap with eartabs pulled down, overshoes and mittens. Then he would light his pipe before he built up the fire in the two stoves.

We let the fire in the cookstove go out about midnight to save on wood. We forgot to empty the water out of the teakettle the first night and it froze solid. The expansion caused it to bulge out at the bottom like a roly poly. After this it would rock, roll, jig and whistle at the same time when it got hot, which really amused us kids. Often our food started to freeze right on the table before we finished eating. We always said grace at the table, both before and after meals. The three of us took turns and one time when it was Ole's turn he folded his little hands and began, *"I Jesus navn gaar ve til bords"* then started to cry saying, "I'm cold Mama." We all three piled into bed and got warm while Mama warmed up the food again. This time we put on our mittens and coats and finished our dinner.

We used to keep a supply of rocks in the oven. These, when hot, made a good footwarmer when slipped into a man's wool sock and took the place of a heating pad we did not have.

Christmas was a very bleak affair for us that year. My parents must have felt it even worse than us kids. They promised us a wonderful tree and everything next year when we got really settled and we were optimistic and looked forward to it. Santa could not possibly find his way in such weather and we thought it was better that he had stayed home and not taken any chances of getting lost. We knew that our sisters had presents for us when the mail could get through. That wouldn't be until it warmed up and the road had been broken through, which the neighbors told us might not be until spring. We had the pups and the kitten to play with, and two hens. The other hens and the rooster had frozen to death. We took these two remaining hens into the house and kept them in a coop. Our potatoes and vegetables were like stones. After they froze hard, we put them all out in the snowbank and brought in just what we wanted to eat each day. We poured cold water over them; this drew the frost out, which formed a thick coating of ice like a shell around them. When we burst this off, we could then peel and cook them. They had a peculiar, sweet taste but it was all we had, so we ate them without a whimper.

The most peculiar thing about this winter was that not a single one of us had the slightest sign of a cold. We had given up hope of ever getting the place we first cancelled, so we had to look for a new location. According to the township maps, there were several quarter-sections of open land about ten miles east of where we were, so Papa set out afoot to look the land over and pick out the one he considered the best and most suitable.

Papa then went to Castor and filed. He borrowed a saddlehorse for this trip, as it was forty miles away. The snow and slush made walking difficult and the oxen were too slow. Castor was at the end of the railroad at that time. Whenever the weather would permit, Papa drove up to our new homestead and worked on a house for us. This was a dugout in the sidehill; just a temporary place to move into until we could build something permanent. We had to have some kind of a place in which to live before we could move.

We loved to go over to Vickres' to play with Lizzie and Franz, who were our own age. As I have mentioned before, it was a most hospitable place and one could generally find a crowd there. They all spoke Norwegian and some Minnesota English; we learned that, too. We had strict orders from home to speak only Norwegian. Whenever we went to Caseleyville after the mail, Mrs. Caseley took it upon herself to correct our pronunciation if she caught us using words not in line with perfect English. This we were grateful for and all three of us came through without any decided accent, other than a purely Canadian one. Mrs. Caseley owned a lot of cattle, as well as horses, and was one of the earliest settlers in the community.

Alec Johnson, our nearest neighbor, was a real old timer. The first time we called on him, we were sitting quietly listening to him telling us how to make the best sourdough pancakes, after I had inquired about what was in the little lard pail hanging by a wire from the ceiling above the cookstove. All of a sudden, we heard a hen cackle. Looking up, I spied two apple boxes hanging on the wall with a hen in each. One hen had laid an egg, which he gave us to take home. That was the only fresh egg we had that winter and my first experience with caged layers.

Chapter III

It was a joyful day when Sina came home from Camrose for a visit. It is difficult to imagine the tremendous admiration and love we had for our older sisters. We just could not leave her alone for a minute during the day and we had to draw straws to see which one of us got to sleep with her first. I am sure she would have enjoyed her night's rest much better by herself. The single bed that Papa had made for her was fashioned with a canvas bottom that stretched and was deep in the center like a hammock. One person could manage comfortably but two were wedged tight. That made no difference to us for we would have slept on sticks and stones just to be near her and she didn't have the heart to protest.

While she was at home, one of the strangest things happened and I have wondered about it many times since. One evening our cow happened to break loose and got away without us knowing in which direction she went. Sina took a rope and started out to hunt for her, with me along for company. We headed for the big coulee where we saw a few head of cattle. There was also a large herd grazing across the creek in the distance. Our cow was trained to come when we called her, for she knew she would get some oats, so she nearly always answered us with a real bawl. She was a heavy milker and would no doubt have come home by herself when her udder began to pain her. All this we didn't know, then.

We called and called, but got no answer and no cow could we find. Finally we decided to cross the creek and take a look at the bunch over there. We found a place where the water was quite shallow and enough rocks had been rolled into the water to make some kind of crossing. We managed to step from one to the next without getting our feet wet. We hiked on to look for our cow in the herd we could see, without finding any trace of her. By the time we started back it was getting dark and we got lost. We could not even find the place where we had crossed the creek before. The water seemed much deeper now but we knew that we must get to the other side somehow. We walked up and down that rough creek bed until Sina got the idea to tie the rope around me, right under my arms, and told me to wade in and see how deep it was. If it were too deep, she would pull me back to safety with the rope. I remember well how awfully cold it was but I managed to wade through water up to my waist. When I got over to the other side, I held on to the rope while she waded across.

When we got to the top of the coulee bank again, we thought that we could see our light and we headed in that direction. When we got home, soaking wet and shivering, Sina said, "If it hadn't been for the lantern on the roof, we would never have found our way home." Mama looked a little pale and said, "God must have put one up there to guide you, for this morning when Papa went to work on the house, he took ours with him." In the middle of the night we heard that familiar bawl again and Mama got up and milked the cow and tied her securely. We never discussed the incident much but it left us with a kind of peculiar feeling.

Spring finally came and with it renewed hope. We had, at least, summer and warm weather to look forward to.

It was a lovely, sunshiny day on the 28th of March, 1911, when we again loaded our belongings into the covered wagon and headed east. This day was a happy one for all of us. We were glad to get away to a new start. It is characteristic of the pioneer to always look ahead, to hope and plan for the future. The great faith we had in the country was never shaken, in spite of the trials and setbacks we had experienced. Time, as nothing else, enables one to gain a keener insight into the real purpose of adventure, such as pioneering. I have found that the chief requirements are faith to start with and fortitude to carry on. Applied in an intelligent manner, these two are priceless ingredients for success.

March is an ugly time of the year in Alberta. The grass has not yet turned green and there are still dirty snowdrifts lodged in the brush around the sloughs and along the roadside. We passed many herds of cattle and horses. At that time this was purely a ranching country with no roads to follow except buffalo trails that led to a waterhole or a spring. We made our own trail and the same one was used for many years by other settlers who came in later.

We were headed for the southeast quarter of Section 22, township 36, range 8, west of the 4th meridian. There were no fences, houses or markers of any kind to guide us. It was just a vast, rolling range covered with dry prairie wool and a few poplar bluffs, here and there. I had my kitten caged in the humpty-dumpty egg crate on top of the load. The two hens, in their coop, were occupying their old place at the back. The puppies were busy chasing gophers and would run ahead of the wagon, then come back to see if we were still coming, as if trying to urge us on.

We pulled into camp about dusk. It was only a one room dugout in the sidehill but soon the kettle was boiling and Mama brought out one of her best white tablecloths, covered the rough table and said, "Children, let us be thankful. We are home at last."

After supper we made our beds. We were quite enthused over the idea of sleeping in bunks and all three of us wanted the top bunk. I had to give in and let the boys have it. Our feather beds came to the rescue again as both springs and mattresses and we soon had a most comfortable place to sleep; moreover it was warm. We began to realize that we were tired and I can still remember the contented feeling that crept over me as I dozed off to sleep that first night.

Our first big problem was to get water. Right after breakfast the next morning we decided where we wanted a well and started digging a hole four feet square. When we got down to six feet we had to erect a tripod, which was three poles tied together at the top with a pulley attached plus a rope for a bucket to haul up the dirt. This is where us kids' job started. The clay was heavy and it took all three of us, hand over hand, to get the filled bucket up, then two to hold it while the third one would swing the bucket to the side and pour out the contents. I remember dropping the bucket once. We were mighty glad just then that there was no ladder up that well! Towards evening we noticed that the clay was beginning to stick to the bucket and before long we could see the water come bubbling up. The next morning it was within four feet of the top and very good water. The strange part of it is that we dug wells all over the place for the next twenty years and spent hundreds of dollars for drilling and boring holes but this was the only good water we found and this same well is still in use today.

The next thing was to get a fireguard around the house. This was done by plowing a square of about ten furrows close to the shack and two more on the outside of the first, some distance apart. In case the fire would jump the first, we could backfire between the other two and be able to check the fire that way. Prairie fires were a real threat in those days and the last thing we did before going to bed each night was for someone to climb up the hill and make sure there was no prairie fire in sight.

Right away after the fireguard was finished, Papa began to get some land broken and seeded to oats, so as to have some feed for the animals. There were a great number of rocks to be picked before one could plow and that was another job for us kids. We managed to get eleven acres broken and seeded that spring.

It was our intention to build a house as soon as possible; the little dugout in the sidehill was just a temporary place for us to stay. We finally decided on a site in the southeast corner of our quarter where we had a fine view of the surrounding countryside. When more settlers came in we would be able to see their buildings. It was hoped they would do the same. Before long, the cellar was dug. Since there was no lumber to be had within forty miles and no money to buy it with, there was no alternative but sod. We knew that we could get plenty of logs in Nose Hills, so we decided to start hauling logs right away. It was seven miles to the hills and it took two days to make the round trip. I used to love these trips to the hills. We took two teams of oxen with two wagons. Two of us got to go along to drive the one team, the third had to stay home to help Mama. We each took our turn and I was always glad when it came my turn to go.

There were no settlers in the hills at that time. We roamed about wherever we liked, cooked over a campfire and slept under the stars. When saskatoons were ripe, we were at a loss where to start picking; the hills seemed literally one mass of berries. We drove up and made camp by noon the first day and started chopping down the trees. As soon as we had cut enough for the two loads, we kids snaked them up the coulee bank with an ox each as fast as Papa could get them trimmed. All we used was a logging chain fastened to a single tree and wrapped around one end of the log. Papa would finish loading both wagons before he built the campfire and cooked our supper. We had an old coffee pot that we called Blacky which we took with us on these trips. It was black as coal from the smoke it had been subjected to while hanging on a tripod over an open fire. The coffee made in this manner was extra special, I thought.

Once in a while, Papa would rake the coals and get out the old tin frying pan and make some of the biggest flapjacks I have ever seen. I used to sit, fascinated, as he flipped the cakes twice, and occasionally three times, before they hit the pan again. We loved to sit around the campfire at night and listen to stories and the many weird noises of the wilderness. The next morning we got up early to pick saskatoons. The three of us could pick enough to fill a washtub by noon. These berries made excellent fruit juice or wine. We had no way of preserving them other than making juice, which we enjoyed all winter. We made it home early enough to get the wagons unloaded before supper and get set for another trip to the hills the next day.

We were all summer working on our house. There were other things that had to be done, such as putting up hay for the cattle, weeding the garden and picking rock. We were glad to change jobs occasionally, as building a sod house is no fun. The frame of our house was of logs. These were hewed flat on one side and were placed upright and close together, which made a nice solid surface to tack paper onto. The sod had to be tough, so that it would hold together. This was not hard to find and we measured every piece with a yardstick to be exactly thirty-two inches long, after Papa broke the sod with our sixteen inch plow. We used an old hand saw to saw the edges straight. In this way every sod was the same size. We laid one layer crosswise, the next lengthwise on top and filled in the cracks between sods with loose dirt, so as to make it windproof. For the roof we laid poles close together with a thick layer of slough-grass, then tar paper, and covered it with a solid layer of sod.

A sod house has the distinction of being cool in summer and warm in winter. That is about the only distinctive feature about it that I can vouch for, except that it made a good backstop for passed balls. Every time we missed the baseball, it would sink into the sod wall with a thud and leave an impression. There were dozens of these holes on the north side of our soddy and a stranger once asked what made all the "pock marks" on the wall.

One way to seal cracks in a sod wall and make it windproof is to wait until the thermometer registers thirty below zero or more, then throw water up against it a number of times. The water freezes and forms a coat of ice. To paper a sod house, one would drive numerous wooden pegs into the sod at regular intervals, then nail a tack through the paper into the pegs. The paper will hang securely. I learned this through curiosity; one place where I was visiting I saw hundreds of bright, shiny tacks all over the wall and upon inquiring how they got there I was shown how by peeking through a crack in the paper.

One of the biggest worries a homesteader had at that time was to have enough food to last all winter. We needed two windows and some nails to complete the house. Our provisions were getting low too so Papa decided to drive to Castor with the oxen. Our grocery order read like this: Six hundred pounds of flour, one hundred of sugar, one hundred of oatmeal, twenty-five pounds of coffee, fifty of salt, one ten pound box each of dried apples, peaches, apricots and prunes, two kegs of salt herring and six pounds of casino smoking tobacco, besides matches and coal oil.

We had prunes for breakfast every morning and we were rationed to three prunes only. The reason: so we would not tire of them. On many occasions we were tempted to fill our dish when no one was looking but we didn't and, to this day, when I eat prunes, I invariably think of this and limit myself to just three.

It took four days to make the trip to Castor. Papa always brought each of us a small bag of hard candy when he came home. We did not look for nor expect anything else. This time, besides the grocery order, he brought a big wooden barrel and an old trunk. We were curious to know what was in the trunk and were rather disappointed when we discovered it was full of old books of every kind. He had traded his pearl-handled revolver for a shotgun, an empty barrel and a trunk full of old books.

We moved into the new sod house as soon as the windows were in. Geese and ducks were coming down from the north by the hundreds every day and the air was crisp and chilly in the mornings. Fall was here and cold weather was creeping up on us fast. We still didn't have a place for our cattle, so we set to work to complete the sod barn we had started. By now we were experienced in the art and it went along much faster, since we didn't have to be particular about filling the cracks as we had done in the house. For several days we worked; it was so hazy that we could barely see the sun through the dense air. We worked with eartabs turned down and fur collars up, with mittens and wool socks on.

The north wind was really stinging our faces as we placed the last sod on the roof. Soon the snowflakes came tumbling down in a blinding fury; strange, as if old winter had held off as long as he could, then let loose with all his might. Only a homesteader can know the satisfaction that comes with having a warm house, plenty to eat and a place for his animals, when a blizzard rages outside.

We had worried with the oxen all summer, trying to break them to ride. They were dangerous and we took the most chances with them, yet somehow we never seemed to get hurt. We gradually learned their traits and they are different, same as humans. To get on their backs we had to stand on something and jump, for they were much too tall for us to make it from the ground. So we hit upon the idea to train them to hold their heads down. In this way we could lie across their necks and, when they lifted their heads, it was easy to climb on their backs and get settled. To begin with, one of us would hold their heads down, while the other climbed on and before long they got the idea and lowered their heads on their own accord, as soon as we took hold of their ears or horns. They got the best of us many a time, and we landed head over heels. We soon learned to stay with them and they learned to tolerate us in a way. Our daily ride to the water hole was good training. They went there without any guiding; it was useless to try, for an ox is the most stubborn of animals and goes his own way.

We had four by now. Old Bill was blind in one eye; Dick was the tricky one and was forever trying some way to get rid of us. He would hit for the densest brush patch to see if he could rub us off or for the open barn door. We played a dangerous game often; two of us got on his back and when he hit for the open door we waited until he was just outside, then the one in front would say, "Jump." We both threw our right leg over his back at the same time and slid to the ground, always in the nick of time. Tom was the fastest one. He never tamed like the others and we had to use a line on him since he was very nervous. He would run right along with only a kick in the ribs.

Sometimes they would get away from us and into a herd of cattle. It was then a big problem to catch them without a saddlehorse. Once when old Bill ran off with a herd of range cattle, Papa drove the team of oxen, hitched to the wagon, into the herd. Martin jumped out and sneaked up on his blind side, got hold of his neck strap, then clamped his cap over Bill's good eye. This blinded the ox temporarily, stopping him long enough for Martin to get hold of the ring in his nose. Old Bill was furious when he found he was caught.

As soon as the folks gained enough confidence in our ability to handle the oxen and some assurance that they were not aiming to kill us, we amused ourselves immensely by practising different kinds of stunts on them. Bill, whose back was real flat, was the main attraction for our experiments. One day at the waterhole, we hit upon the idea to pretend that he was a three masted prairie schooner. All three of us climbed on, standing straight up and holding on to each other. We sang "Over the Bounding Main" at the top of our voices as we ambled toward home. What we lacked in harmony we made up in volume, to the annoyance of the ox, as he kept flapping his ears back and forth and shaking his head. We were having a fine time until we spied Mama hurrying toward us, frightened to death, thinking one or all of us had been massacred. She took the wind out of our sails, so to speak, and we had to think up a different stunt for the next time.

Our cow Guro was inclined to be somewhat temperamental.

This we knew but did not realize to what extent until we got the harness on her and were ready to hitch her to the stoneboat to haul a barrel of water from the well in the pasture. Papa was away plowing with the oxen at the time and we were tired of having to make several trips to the well every day with a bucket to get water for the house. It was a quarter of a mile and we could see no reason why the cow could not be put into service and save us that much work. We did not consult Mama as to the feasibility of the idea, for we were somewhat dubious as to her reaction. However, we thought we could manage without her finding out.

Guro did not like the arrangement. To be on the safe side, we put two ropes around her horns with one of us on each side holding on. In that way we kept her between us in case she got the notion to attack. She already had the notion and we had a wild west show all by ourselves. The only time that we made any headway was when she took after one or the other of us that happened to be in front of her. The barrel rolled off the stoneboat and almost hit me and from then on her sole idea was to get even with us. We finally got close enough to a fence post to get a hitch around it and snub her tight. We managed to get the harness off her and carry it back to the barn. We retrieved the water barrel and got our buckets and started for the well. We made two trips before we dared to turn her loose. At milking time, Mama was wondering why the cow acted so strange and she gave only half the usual amount of milk. None of us said a word but I thought I could see a peculiar glint in her eyes that night as she tucked us into bed, all three too tired to finish our supper.

Mama must have had a hard time getting used to the way of life on the prairie. She had known better times than we could possibly hope for on the homestead. She cautioned us repeatedly to hold on to what culture we had inherited and no matter how far we were from people or civilization, never to let ourselves down. Some of the things she impressed on me will always be remembered and have been a guiding force in the right direction all my life. One of these had to do with temptation. She said, "If you are tempted to do a thing, stop a minute and ask yourself, 'Is this good for me?' You can tell. Then judge accordingly. Do what you know to be right and you will end up being proud of yourself." She was a truly religious person and always made the best of whatever happened. She insisted on a white tablecloth for every day, even if it was made of flour sacks with a little embroidery in the corners.

It gave a touch of festivity to a meal. On Sunday she brought out the good linen one and we always said grace before and after meals. She repeatedly stressed the importance of good manners, no matter where we happened to be.

She took great delight in explaining the beauty of lightning. We would go outside and watch the intricate flashes play all over the heavens and she would stand fascinated as it lit up the entire sky. I suspect that it was done partly to keep us from becoming frightened if we were caught out in a thunderstorm. I still like to go outside and watch the clouds roll by when a storm is in the air and have no fear of the weather.

Afternoon coffee was a tradition with our family. We younger ones had to add some extra milk to ours but nevertheless it was coffee and we relished it along with a big sandwich, cake or cookies, whatever was on hand. I have often wondered what made me grow so much taller than any of my sisters. They all gave credit to the good Canadian air. I suspect that my keen appetite and zest for food had quite a bit to do with it. At any rate, I have been the object of much teasing. To make me even more conscious of my height, I managed to acquire the nickname of Shorty. This has stayed with me down through the years and even now I find myself answering to that moniker.

This had been a good year with plenty of rain and our oats turned out wonderful. After the crop was cut and stooked, we had to stack the bundles, as there was no threshing machine anywhere around. They were so heavy and full of grain it was all we kids could do to lift one. It took two of us to pull them around on the stack. We tried to build a round stack with a bulge in the middle, then taper it off to a peak at the top to shed rain. We had six large stacks when we finished and each one looked different. One in particular resembled a statue of an old man. Papa did all the heavy lifting. The price of oats at that time was eleven cents a bushel, which would not have paid us to have them threshed, so we fed them to the stock like they were.

We had put up a lot of hay during the summer, both slough and upland; the latter was called prairie wool and it is one of the best and most nutritious grasses that grow. It has a grain in it and instead of drying up and dying in winter like most grasses, it cures on the roots. Horses especially will paw through the snow to get it. I learned to manipulate the hay rake this summer. Driving the oxen, it was difficult to get the rake to trip right, they being too slow. We had to have a whip in our hand at all times or they would stop in their tracks. The only way to work it, we found, was to whip and trip at the same time; if our timing was right, it worked fine.

To build a civilization is neither fast nor an easy job. Survival is the important factor and to this end nature can assist or retard progress. The homesteader's own initiative and that of his family can overcome a lot of reversals, and did. We were now snowed in for the winter. Drifts of snow were piled up in our yard. We shovelled paths to the barn and other places, which gave us kids the exercise we needed and it was fun. Our education had been neglected during the summer and now we had to make up for it. Papa supervised our reading and arithmetic. Mama was responsible for our religious training. We studied Bible history and catechism until we could recite them by heart. We were so far away from churches and civilization such as we had been used to, yet strangely so close to God. We had the impression that there was no one between us and God and confided in Him as if it were another person, a super being that would grant us our wishes if that wish were for our own good. In my wanderings over the prairie I would sometimes lose my direction. Instead of getting panicky I would climb the nearest high hill and ask God how to get home. Invariably I would spot a familiar landmark and find my way back. I kept such incidents to myself, as it seemed natural to me that others did the same thing in an emergency.

We dug into the old trunk for additional subject matter. Here we found a veritable gold mine of information and the basis of our education. There was fiction and fairy tales, ancient history, literature, poetry and political speeches; in fact, most everything. Geography lessons were most interesting. My parents took turns to describe the different countries we happened to be studying and often told of real experiences they had in some of these places. We skipped the English alphabet entirely. Somehow we had learned to read without it. We kept asking what this or that word meant and in that manner soon learned enough words to make sense out of a story. We had to speak English as much as we knew how but quite often we came to a dead end and had to resort to Norwegian to explain ourselves. Mama always addressed us in Norwegian, lest we forget our mother tongue.

We had our daily chores to look after and were as eager as any school kids to get out into the fresh air. First we had to bundle up. The intense cold is hard on the lungs and you don't have to be told not to run, for you know it from the way you feel. We soon found out what the big barrel was for. It was placed behind the stove and had to be kept full of snow to melt for soft water. We hauled water from the well to cook with and that barrel had to be left outside until a couple inches of ice froze on top, so that we could roll it into the house; if left outside, it would freeze solid. There were many big snowdrifts around our yard from which we sawed blocks of snow and hauled them on our sled to the kitchen for the soft water barrel.

This gave us ideas about building a snowhouse. After one of our history lessons on Eskimos we decided to build an igloo. It went fine until we were putting the last few blocks on the roof, when all of a sudden it caved in and almost buried us.

We also knew the feel of a cross-cut saw on a log. I can still hear the ringing sound of it as we pulled it back and forth on a frozen poplar pole, one at each end, the third sitting on top to hold it down. When he got too cold we would change off. This green wood was excellent to hold fire in the heating stove all night long. It took a lot of wood to keep us going and we had to work at it every day for a while.

It was now December and the thought of Christmas and Santa Claus was uppermost in our minds. We remembered what our parents had promised us last year; also, that Santa got lost and never did find us and that we were even further away and harder to find this year. Our parents assured us that he knew where we lived and for us just to be good kids and he would be sure to come. We were not too sure about it and after talking it over among ourselves, we decided to put up a few landmarks and not take any chances.

When the time came to bring in the Christmas tree, you can imagine our surprise when we saw the bare twigs of a dry willow tree set in a bucket of stones to keep it standing upright. Mama seemed to be enjoying herself as we watched her pull white cotton from a comforter and cover each branch, then spread a pile to look like a blanket of snow underneath to conceal the bucket. Strings of roseberries that we had gathered in the fall made lovely streamers and icicles made of tinsel from the lining of casino smoking tobacco packages looked real. We saved all kinds of colored paper during the year and from this she made little baskets to hold home-made candy. Then there were lots of big, round sour cream cookies with our names written on them with beet juice hanging here and there. All this, together with a box of Christmas candles she had brought from Norway, made one of the most memorable Christmas trees I have ever seen and one I shall never forget.

We had a hard time getting to sleep that night. It was so wonderful: the Christmas tree in the middle of the floor, covered with snow and all those pretty things hanging on every branch; the *Julekake* that Mama had baked; *Fattigman* and *Serina Kaker*, each in different tins, waiting to be eaten on Christmas Day. Once in a while, Mama would come in to see if we were asleep and tiptoe out again. We thought we heard some bells outside. Ole jumped up to see if it were Santa and he found it was snowing some. Then we must have fallen asleep.

On Christmas morning we woke up bright and early. It was still dark but we could not wait for daylight to come, so we lit the coal oil lamp and right there under the tree stood three brand new homemade sleds, and for each of us, a set of homeknit mittens and scarf to match. Mine were a lovely American Beauty color which somehow resembled the color of the writing on the cookies. Mine were knit in an intricate design; the boys' were plain and light grey. We were anxious to get outside and try our new sleds but not before breakfast, we were told.

Besides, we had to sing the traditional julesongs. In Norway we always joined hands and circled the tree while we sang. Our favorites were *Jeg er saa glad ver julekveld* and *Glade Jul*. Mama and Papa joined us and after this we bundled up and went out to sleighride. It was forty below zero and, although we were used to being outside every day, one never got quite used to that kind of cold. The sleigh riding was wonderful. We had a perfect place to slide, close enough to the house so that occasionally we could run in to get warm. We were well acquainted with frostbite and watched each other's faces for signs of white patches. We would then rub some snow on that particular place to get circulation started. We did not run to the house every time but kept on at whatever we were doing. We remembered the birds at Christmas, too, by tying a bundle of oats to the clothesline pole. It was surprising to see how many snowbirds gathered to celebrate.

It was one of those mornings when the whole white world lay crisp and still. Hoarfrost hung on the taut clothes line. And on the trees around the slough the sun shone with a cold glittering sparkle. A few rabbit tracks criss-crossing around the yard was the only intrusion on Nature's perfect picture.

Chapter IV

Our house was divided into two rooms: kitchen and one large living room-bedroom combined. Later, when we had time and material, we intended to divide this room again. We had only one heating stove, consequently we all had to be within range of it to keep from freezing. We had just enough lumber for one floor, so this had to go on the kitchen, since there was a cellar underneath. For floor in the big room, we hauled in clean oat straw and tramped it down solid to a thickness of about six inches before putting down the rugs which we had brought with us from Norway. It was lucky that we had these for they cheered up the place with their colorful patterns, besides making our floor warm and soft.

The winter evenings were long and we had to think up different ways of entertaining ourselves besides reading. A solid diet of literature and study can get boring. For diversion, Papa brought out a deck of cards and was going to teach us how to play Norwegian whist. This, I suspect, was for his own amusement as well as ours. Mama did not altogether approve of cards, and could not tell an ace from a deuce, but agreed to let us try it. They got a real surprise when they found out that all three of us were quite expert at the game and finally we had to confess that we had learned to play cards at Vickres. From then on we had a regular foursome, Ole and I against Martin and Papa. Papa was so anxious to make good players out of us that he supervised every play and would reprimand us if we missed a trick. The height of our ambition was to set him and this we managed to do once in a while.

Mama would sit and knit and watch. She was an ardent knitter. Sometimes when she ran out of yarn she would unravel something just to knit it all over again. Unfortunately, I did not take after her in this. I did not want a thing to do with knitting needles or crochet hook. She made me learn how and, though I started several scarfs and socks, I don't remember ever finishing one. She finally gave up and did the knitting herself.

Towards the middle of February, a chinook wind comes drifting across the Rockies from the Pacific Ocean. It steals through a pass in the mountain range, then spreads across the prairie like a soothing, comforting warm blanket. Humans and animals alike enjoy the relaxation it brings. Tensions are high during the bitter cold months when Nature is top dog and survival is uppermost in one's mind. The snow begins to melt on the higher spots of ground and the range horses, especially, will stand on these places in groups, resting one hind foot and apparently sleeping during the middle of the day, absorbing the warmth. In winter, they develop a great, long coat of hair and have a shaggy appearance. Their forelock and mane grows long and becomes full of snarls. Their tails almost reach to the ground by spring, when they start shedding. There were great herds grazing around us; we knew which ranch they belonged to by their brand. They would paw through the snow for their food all winter and eat the snow for water. It was surprising how they could survive. Hundreds of them, year after year, came through in good shape without a shelter of any kind except the natural windbreak of a coulee or brush patch.

With cattle it was different. They are not natural rustlers like horses. When a real storm starts brewing they will huddle together in some low spot with their backs to the wind until completely snowed in. That was when the cowboys had to hit the trail, round up the herd and push them to a feeding corral; these were sometimes miles from the ranch and most of the boys would have a little bunkhouse on sleighs with a stove and bed which made a place to crawl into out of the storm. More often they would detour several miles to get to our place to spend the night. In all the years that we were homesteading it never occurred to us to ask any remuneration for food or shelter and none, as I remember, was ever offered.

March seems the longest month of the year and the most dreaded by the ranchers. Weather is changeable; there are warm days that can change into a blinding snowstorm by night. It is this time of year when the weaker animal has a struggle to survive. The snow that melts in February is usually replaced in March, with some added. April ushers in the first sign of spring, when the ice begins to recede from the edges of the sloughs and they begin to fill up with snow water. Soon there are just a few dirt-filled snowdrifts clinging to sidehill brush patches here and there. Then the crocus bursts forth in bloom; the geese and ducks wing their way northward to their mating ground. The appearance of the gopher is a sure sign the winter is over. The jack rabbit will get a different color coat, changing from pure white in winter to a tannish brown in summer, resembling the color of the prairie wool. This is Nature's way of protecting animals. The honk of the first flock of geese in the spring was sweet music to the winter-weary homesteader.

We looked forward to getting our mail regularly during the

summer, which was twice a month. It had to be brought from Castor to Haneyville and Caseleyville along with freight and supplies. Both of these places kept groceries as well as a line of necessities typical of frontier times. It took two days to make the round trip from our place to Caseleyville with the oxen. We had travelled back and forth several times with our Dad the year before. The wagon tracks were still very dim in places and difficult to follow. There were several good landmarks to go by, or so we thought, and we felt sure that we could manage the trip by ourselves now. I, being the oldest, had to do the driving and the boys took turns to accompany me. We felt quite important with our new responsibility and looked forward to the outing and the overnight stay at Vickres.

We sometimes stopped for a while at Shulstads to play with Hyacinth, who was the same age as the boys. On one occasion, Mrs. Shulstad gave us two kittens to take home. We already had a cat and it didn't dawn on us until we were half way home that we might get into trouble by bringing two more kittens. Mama did not like cats; she barely tolerated old Puss, so we decided to turn the kittens loose on the prairie and say nothing about it. When we had travelled about two miles further on, our conscience began to worry us and we turned around and went back to try and find them. This took longer than we anticipated and by the time we found the cats, the sun was low on the horizon. We were usually home by this time and, just as the sun went down, we could see the silhouette of a man on top of a hill not so far away. That was our Dad, afoot, coming to look for us. He looked rather pale and asked what had happened. We told him the cat story and he told us that Mama was sick with worry and that we must never tarry like that again. They were so glad to find that we were not hurt that the cats were forgotten. This was the beginning of our cat ranching and we haven't been without cats since.

We learned to shoot, too, that summer. We had to be very careful and try not to waste any shells. We were interested only in what we could eat and felt bad if we missed a shot. There was an abundance of ducks, prairie chickens and rabbits and duck nests around nearly every slough. We depended on fresh duck eggs for our baking, since we had only one hen left and she didn't lay every day.

We got word that my sisters, Lillie and Martha, were coming home from Bellingham, Washington, and to meet them in Castor. We were so happy to think that we would all be together again. I begged Papa to let me go with him to meet them, as Sina was still working at the National Hotel in Castor and I wanted to see her too.

We started for Castor with Tom and Dick in the covered wagon and went prepared to camp out at night and cook our meals on the road over a campfire. We arrived on the third day. My sisters hardly recognized me; I had grown so tall. I was now twelve years old, tan as a coconut and thin as a beanpole. My thick auburn hair was my main asset. It reached below my waist in two thick braids. I was teased a lot about my green eyes but no freckles at all helped some. The girls had such lovely white complexions. I was such a contrast; having been out in the wind and sun all summer without the thought of a hat, I looked more like an Indian. They started to work on me with face creams and lotions until my face really burned. They tried to wind my braids around my head in some way but I had so much hair that it made me look top heavy. Finally they gave up and accepted me as I was.

We bought the necessary provisions, as far as our finances would allow, and the girls filled in with wonderful presents for us to take home. Castor was just a frontier town at this time but it boasted two excellent hotels, The National and The Cosmopolitan. We stayed at the National, where Sina was working. Lillie was offered a job as a waitress and decided to remain there for a while but Martha was anxious to get home to see Mama and the boys. We allowed one day for visiting and to rest the oxen, then we started homeward again.

The mosquitoes were terrible. We hadn't noticed them quite so much coming down, being fortified against them with a mosquito net on our hats that reached to our shoulders, then tucked under our jackets, long sleeves, gloves and finally brown paper inside my stockings. We were more or less immune to the itching caused by the bites, having been subjected to their attacks for some time, which probably served as an inoculation of some sort. With Martha it was different; she was an easy prey. Her tender white skin, together with her lack of strategy as to how to protect herself, made her a ready target and she was frantic. Knowing the circumstances we had brought the necessary regalia for her to put on. She was reluctant to stoop to such outlandish riggings for fear that some young fellow should come along and see her. She was soon to throw pride to the wind and join our ranks.

The oxen suffered most. When I got tired of riding, I would get out and walk beside them, brushing the mosquitoes off them with willow switches. We had to have a smudge inside the wagon too. We pulled dry grass to burn in an old galvanized pail. Every time we stopped we had to build a smudge for the oxen and often they would try to get right into the middle of it for protection. We had fixed up the tent for Martha to stay in and made it as cozy for her as we knew how. She however was at a loss to cope with some of our doings, we had changed so. When she last saw us we were timid little kids and now we rode wild steers and handled guns like old hunters. We could find our way around the country without fear of getting lost and worked like little beavers at whatever there was to do.

We were also in a quandary as to how to entertain her. She spent most of her time with her crochet work and embroidering things for her hope chest. We decided that was not exciting enough and tried to coax her to go on a crow egg hunt with us and ride the oxen. She kept putting off that expedition until she ran out of excuses and promised that maybe tomorrow she would go along. The day finally came. Martha's first oxback ride is one of the most amusing episodes of my memory. We located some gopher fleas on old Puss, our cat, and decided to take him to Bodi's slough for a swim to drown the fleas. We had to take the oxen to water anyway so we coaxed Martha to come along this time and learn to ride. She had never ridden horseback and was still a little dubious about the idea. We assured her there was nothing to it, no trick at all, besides it was lots of fun, so she agreed to give it a try. Old Bill was the most gentle and tolerant of the oxen. But it was more of a job for her to get on him than we had expected and finally, after much pulling and pushing, she somehow managed to land on him backward. I was holding the cat, who was getting real suspicious by now, and had started to scratch me and wanted to get away. So we turned Bill loose with Martha, scared stiff and with nothing to hold onto, hollering for us to stop him. To top it off, he waded out in the slough and was switching his tail back and forth, splashing water in every direction at her. Ole and I rode double on Dick. We prodded him to get us as far into the water as we could get him to go before the cat got out of hand and I threw him in. He hit the waves with a splash and by leaps and bounds he reached shore, whereupon he beat it for home. We never got a chance to find out how the fleas fared. We got Martha turned around on Bill, finally, and helped her off. We kids laughed so much that we could hardly get on Dick's back. Martha couldn't see the joke right then and we were never able to convince her that there was no trick at all in learning to ride.

She had her boyfriend in the States, and at the end of two months, she went back to Bellingham and got married.

Chapter V

It is much easier for children to adjust to different environments than grown-ups. They have great imagination and I believe we used ours to the fullest. I know we were never bored or at a loss for something to do to amuse ourselves. There were always the ever-present gophers to snare, hundreds of them. They had been unmolested and left to increase in number since time immemorial, except for the few that fell prey to the coyote or fox. There were regular communities of them, we called them gopher hills, and they would run in every direction.

We used to lie still and watch them come out of one hole and run into another as if they were visiting each other. We used a six foot length of binder twine with a slip knot at one end for a snare and, pushing the loop down into the hole about two inches, we would wait for Mr. Gopher to appear. They were pretty game and soon we would see a head sticking out. He would draw back for a minute, then the next time he would come half way up. This was the time to jerk the string and we had him. We sometimes used a double snare for a change. The string had to be twice as long with a loop in the middle. It took two of us, one at each end, to do the trick. We had to be careful and jerk the string at the same time or he would get away; we managed to get one most of the time. At first we were a little timid about killing them. I remember the first big catch we had. We kept putting them in a box until there must have been several dozen. We felt sorry for them and turned them loose. That evening we got a lesson on the destruction they caused to grain and it didn't hurt so much to do away with them after that.

The ant hills were another thing that interested us a great deal. We knew where there were several real large ones. We would sit by the hour and watch the activity and organized routine of the ants; they seemed to always be building or repairing. If an animal happened to step into their hill or demolish it in any way, there was real activity among them at once. Some carried sticks five times their own size and laid them down for, presumably, the carpenter to take over, then hurried back for another and so they kept on. The next time we went to investigate we found the structure back to its original shape.

We had a favorite place fixed up for a playhouse of some sort. This was in a clump of trees around a deep slough not far from the dugout. It was shady and nice and we watched the ducks land on water without our being seen. This way we could observe their natural habits and traits. We got the surprise of our life one day when a pair of the largest white birds we had ever seen flew in and settled on the water; they had the longest red legs and sharpest long beak; I think now that they must have been whooping cranes; however we had never heard of them and the only thing we could think of was the stork. We insisted that not only one but two storks had visited our place, so we waited patiently for the bundle he is supposed to leave. When nothing happened we were really disappointed and we lost faith in the big bird.

One of the earliest visitors we had when we first moved into our big soddy were Mr. & Mrs. Jim Ward. They walked in on us one Sunday morning and introduced themselves. We could tell they were from England by their decided British accent. They worked at the big ranch which later was known as the Circle J. Mrs. Ward did the cooking for twenty to thirty men by herself without any of the conveniences we have today. The ranch was jointly owned by Smith and John, with Mr. Smith as the manager. The Smiths came from the east and were genteel folks with drawing room manners strange to the average cowhand. Quite often on Sunday mornings they would stop by our place while out hunting mushrooms on the prairie. They rode the safest horses and were dressed in their finest; he with white gauntlets and spats, while she wore a lovely hat loaded with flowers and a veil. The wages for the boys working there at this time was one dollar per day, no set hours and the same wage applied to the cook.

The boys from the ranch also used to come down to our place on Sundays for a visit, usually three at a time on horseback. I think they planned it so that each of us would have a saddlehorse to ride around while they were there. This was a real thrill and it didn't take us long to learn to swing into the saddle like a real puncher. They taught us how to balance and hold the reins, also how to get on a spirited horse by cheeking him. This is something that has to be learned by experience and cannot be acquired by listening altogether. The lessons were interesting and gave us a start in the right direction.

They always brought a twenty-two rifle along with plenty of shells for target practice. We thought it wasteful to shoot at a piece of cardboard or tin can. We had to be so careful and make every shell count; they must have got quite a kick out of our marksmanship. We three shot against the three of them and more than held our own. They gave us all the shells that were left each time and told us to practise shooting. The next day we went out hunting gophers and felt pretty bad if we missed a shot.

In the spring of 1912, my Dad got a job of breaking up some land about eight miles from home. He thought it would take him about two weeks. Our supply of groceries was getting rather low but Mama thought we could manage. He took Ole for company and also to make the rations go further. It took him longer than he had first anticipated. We got along fairly well until the end of the third week when we had nothing left but a little flour, salt and one gun shell. We hiked out to a slough on Arthur Wraight's place where we knew there were always a lot of ducks and they were there. I took careful aim, that gun would not hold still, so much depended on that one shot. I fired away but the ducks all flew. We were a discouraged pair of kids when, on the way home, a duck came flying toward us. Martin was carrying the umbrella which we always had to take along in case it should rain, which it seldom did. He threw it at the duck and hit it. The duck fell to the ground stunned. It did not take us long to get it and get home to start it cooking. We had the best duck soup for supper that evening and enjoyed every last bit of it.

We had been gathering duck eggs whenever we came across a nest in which there were some fresh ones. These we used in pancakes. Our luck seemed to have run out, for this was the third day we had hunted and the only thing we found were two hawks' nests. The eggs looked fresh but we broke one to make sure. When we got home, I mixed the pancake batter and hesitated for a while before deciding to use the yolks, the whites I tossed out. We were real hungry and Mama was sick in bed. We both agreed not to tell her about the hawk eggs or she might refuse to eat at all. I made a good-sized stack of the pancakes and she said they tasted real good and praised me for being such a good little cook. I felt real guilty and it was all Martin and I could do to hold down our first and only hawk egg pancakes.

We had come to our wit's end for something to eat. The next morning we set out to find Papa. We cut across country and got to where he was about two o'clock in the afternoon. He had a couple of days' work left and wanted to finish before coming home. After we had eaten our dinner we started for home, taking as much food with us as we could carry. About half way home it started to rain and Martin got so stiff he could hardly walk. Again, the proverbial umbrella came to our rescue. We sat under it until the shower was over, then I took his load as well as my own and Martin held on to one end of the umbrella while I fairly dragged him along. We got home about eight o'clock that night. Mama was frantic with worry about us. She managed to get up and fix us a good meal and got us some dry clothes to put on. I slept until noon the next day without waking; otherwise, we were none the worse for our experience.

In those days one could not go to the store and buy toys like we can today. There were very few on the market; we did not seem to mind the lack of manufactured things. We created our own amusement with what we had at hand, mostly our pets. Our dog Chip was the best play-mate imaginable; most all our activities centered around her. She under-stood two languages equally well; we would talk to her in English, then Mama would tell her the same thing in Norwegian and it did not make a bit of difference, she knew both. She loved to go to town and seemed to know just as well as the rest of us when we were planning a trip. We kept her in the house for at least an hour after Papa left for, if she hap-pened to sneak out on us before that time, she was gone like a shot. Oxen do not travel very fast and she soon caught up with them; she would sneak under the wagon so he wouldn't see her and make her go home. While in town she stayed in the wagon and woe to any man who touched even the side of the box. She was our guardian at all times. When we ventured out on a hunt for crow eggs, we were never afraid of the range cattle for she was always on the alert. Many times when we got quite close to a herd, she started out on her own to chase them away, picking on the bull every time, barking at his head until the herd was on the run, then went to his heels and gave him the chase of his life.

In summer, playing ball was our favorite pastime. We had a bat whittled out of a poplar pole and a rag ball as well as a baseball. Martin was the pitcher, I the catcher and Ole the batter; all we needed was a fielder. As long as we used the rag ball, our dog would retrieve it and sometimes even catch it. We kept a darning needle and thread with us for every once in a while she would get real excited, stop and just tear the ball to pieces. Then I had to get needle and thread and sew it back into shape again before the game could go on. At other times she held it in her mouth and ran in circles teasing us; we had to use real strategy to get it away from her. When we changed to the hard ball she lost all inter-est and refused to play, but as soon as we went back to the rag ball she was back in the game again. We tried hard to get her to stand back where a fielder should but she had her own idea about position and that was just between the pitcher and the catcher. Occasionally one of us tried to field for a change but unless it was a high fly it was useless, for Chip always beat us to it. She was an excellent watch dog, keeping the crows and hawks in the air when they came flying over with intent to pick up one of our chickens. Chasing stray horses or cattle that might accidentally drift into the yard was her self-appointed job. One time when we had butchered a pig and it came time for coffee, Papa told her to watch the meat. She lay down beside it and, while we all went in the house, one of our neighbors happened along and in spite of her warnings he touched the meat. She bit him on the finger and he talked about shooting her, so we kids forgot about lunch, got her in the house and hid her under the bed until he had gone home.

We had plenty of rain this summer; the sloughs and lakes were full of water, so it was decided that we should learn to swim. Our Dad was an excellent swimmer and naturally we would take after him. Not having any bathing suits we supplemented with old overalls. As soon as we landed at the designated slough, Papa dived in and gave us an exhibition that would do credit to a champion. When it came our turn it was different, for we just didn't have the knack. He pointed to the dog who swam all around us and hadn't had a single lesson; we were ashamed to think a dog was smarter than we were and even though we tried very hard it was to no avail. The lack of know-how, together with those overalls full of water, caused us to sink to the muddy bottom. At the end of our sojourn, we had to line up on the beach and splash water on each other to get enough mud off us and the overalls to make it home. We decided, then and there, that we were landcrabs and swimming was not for us. Papa, who was not endowed with all the patience in the world, was real disgusted with us and walked home by himself.

We used to enjoy going along with him to visit some of our bachelor neighbors; sometimes we managed to take them by surprise. If they happened to see us coming they would grab the broom and make the dust fly. Many times we have been met at the door with a cloud of dust. They always had plenty of food, with most of it sitting on the table in jars and cans. One could be sure to find the coffee pot, as well as a heap of egg shells, at the back of the stove. Some kept their egg shells in the warming closet then, when dry, crushed them up for the few laying hens as a supplement for oyster shells. The bed was usually made but the dishes were most often left until later. In fact, I knew one man who, when he was so busy in the field that he could not find time to bother with dishes, would keep a tub of water under the table and drop them in after every meal, until he ran out of clean ones and had to start washing. Hospitality was one thing that was not lacking in any way; one was always welcome.

Most bachelor shacks were real small; they were meant to be just temporary quarters; some place to get into, so as to have a roof over their heads while they got settled. Quite often, it was years before they managed to build on. There was some advantage in having such cramped quarters, for they could sit at the table and reach anything on the stove or cupboard for that matter, if they had one. At threshing time, when a crew of men had to be fed, there was barely standing room. One fellow I know very well had to take his bed outside before he could serve the threshers their dinner. For a makeshift table, he brought in two saw-horses and the door to his coal shed. Thus, with newspaper for a tablecloth and a few apple boxes to sit on, they made out fine. The food was excellent and that was the main thing. No one seemed to have much to grumble about in those days. The future belonged to those who looked forward to it with optimism and took advantage of present opportunity. This same homesteader later became a prosperous farmer with a lovely family and a beautiful home.

George Henwood was a bachelor and one of the earliest settlers in our district. He lived in a soddy just below Nose Hills. We used to stop and chat awhile with him every time we went by his place to the hills for wood. The first visit I remember very well. We had forgotten to fill our water keg at home and, seeing a curbed well in his yard complete with rope and pulley, we knew instinctively that there was water in it. He was glad to see us and helped pull up the bucket of water from the deep well. He did not however offer us a cool drink. We got a real shock when we sat down to eat our lunch and, incidentally, quench our thirst. The first swallow nearly gagged us for it was equal to a double dose of epsom salts. We found out later that he could not use the water himself. We never did know for sure if he was just trying to play a joke on us, since we didn't mention it to him.

We stopped many a time after that but always made sure to bring our own drinking water with us. He had the most peculiar arrangement for sleeping quarters that I have ever seen. His bed was built right across one end of his shack and was twelve feet long with a board partition in the middle. He slept in one end and kept the other end for company. It had poplar poles for bottom and heaps of clean straw for mattress; this had an advantage since it could be renewed easily. The wooden floor reached only to the edge of the bed; he probably ran out of lumber, as under the bed was just dirt floor. George was a prosperous farmer in his day. He had the first car in the community, a model T Ford, which was the envy of some and a great deal of pleasure to others who took advantage of his generosity. He also had a great number of horses and one of the finest farms in the community, still he would not give up his soddy but kept living in it until he had to give up farming because of old age. His great hobby was cards. He used to come to our place often for a game of five hundred or bridge; his real love, however, was poker and many a good load of wheat as well as many a good night's sleep was lost over the blue chips.

The last time I saw George was at the Old Men's Home in Youngstown. He was quite feeble by now and was lying down on his bed but when I entered he made a valiant effort to stand and almost fell. I asked him what he did to amuse himself and his eyes glowed like to diamonds and he went through the motion of dealing a five card poker hand.

Chapter VI

The Railroad was extending eastward and we heard rumors that towns were springing up along the line. The main one was already named Coronation. The C.P.R. built the towns on their own land. Since they owned half of the country it was an easy matter for them to locate on their own property. This new townsite was eighteen miles west of our place. Already there was building going on; a fine hotel was under construction as well as a livery barn and bank. My sisters wrote from Castor that they had been promised jobs as waitresses in this hotel, so would come home for Christmas and a vacation while it was being completed. This job would bring them much closer to home and we were so happy over that. We changed our post office to Wheatbelt now, since the railroad survey showed that there would be a town somewhere near to it. This was nine miles southwest. Bob Wilson kept a store and post office and we could get provisions at the same time that we went for the mail.

We had to blaze a new trail and often it was difficult to follow the same tracks we had made the time before. The country was rough and rolling with a lot of sloughs and rocks to dodge as well as the ever-present badger holes. One day, about two weeks before Christmas, Papa and I got up real early and started out for Wheatbelt. I was to do some shopping for Mama: hard candies, popcorn and such to hang on the tree. We also had two big parcels coming, one from Eaton's and one from Simpson's. We knew they would be at the post office for we had sent the orders over a month before. We did not dare leave our shopping until the last minute. December is a tricky month; if a blizzard were to descend on us, we would have to wait until the weather moderated, be that a week or a month. The thermometer registered fifteen below zero this day, which was considered quite mild for this time of year. The day was rather murky; we could barely see the sun at noon. We always put plenty of straw in the bottom of the sleigh as well as several quilts and the foot warmer.

We got everything we had come for, including those precious parcels, and started out for home. About half way it began to snow and before we knew it we could not see ten feet ahead of us; it came down in a blinding fury that made visibility nil. The oxen were stubborn and wanted to go in the wrong direction, or so it seemed. Papa got out and walked beside them and tried to guide them the best he could. He finally admitted that he was lost and climbed back into the sleigh and tied the lines. They immediately turned around and headed right into the wind and put their heads to the ground and hauled us up and down into sloughs and over hills. We had our heads covered and only when we thought we were going to tip over did we jump up.

This kept on for several hours, until we had given up hope of finding home that night. Our only hope was that we might come across a shelter somewhere that we could get into for the night and out of this blizzard. We were sitting in the bottom of the sleigh covered up the best we could, huddled together to keep warm, when all of a sudden the oxen stopped. We peeked out to see what had happened and right there in front of us was the dim glow of a lantern in the room of our own house. The boys were all dressed and ready to unhitch and take care of the oxen.

We were stiff with cold but inside was warmth and food and hot coffee waiting for us; it was wonderful to be home safe and we were all so thankful. An ox has a wonderful sense of direction. We learned that, left to find their own way, they will go against the worst storm to get home, where a horse will not buck a storm but will turn tail and drift with it.

The next day, Mr. Bucknell, a homesteader, came to sell beef. He offered a lovely hind quarter that weighed around two hundred pounds, for ten dollars. He told us not to worry about paying for it until spring, so we enjoyed beef all winter. We learned the next summer that one of his oxen had fallen into a well and broken his neck just before Christmas.

The big catalogues from Eaton's and Simpson's were our wonderland. We never tired of looking and pretending, when in reality we knew we would not be able to get the pretty things we picked out. Guns and traps fascinated us tremendously. During the winter, trapping coyotes and weasels was a great pastime, for there were plenty of both species around our farm. We were too young to try for the coyote, so we set some gopher traps and soon began to catch the weasels or white ermine, as they are called. We learned to skin and stretch the hides. When they were ready to ship, we packed them neatly in a box and sent them to a furrier in Winnipeg. When the returns came, it was for twenty-five cents for average, to sixty-five for the large, perfect ones. We caught about fifty in a season, which was the only way we had of making any spending money.

In later years we trapped a lot of coyotes but one really has to know how to trap them as they are very cunning and suspicious. The badger was another fur animal that we used to good purpose. There was no sale for the skins but we utilized them to good advantage by lining our caps, mittens and moccasins. We tanned the hides. Then, to get them soft enough to stitch through, we had to rub the skinside with pumice stones and pull them back and forth over a saw-horse until pliable. We spent a lot of our time outside and I thank the badger skins for keeping us from freezing during the intense cold weather we experienced while doing our daily chores. One of these was to take the cattle to water to a slough about a mile away. We each rode an ox while Papa walked and carried the ax to cut a hole through the ice. This hole had to be cut every day, as it froze solid again overnight, sometimes to two or three feet in thickness.

In winter, when we wanted to go skating, we went out to a slough somewhere with a broom to sweep off the snow and cleared a place on the ice big enough to skate. This we had to do after every snow-storm. I sometimes drift off mentally, thinking about snow. There are different kinds of snow; it varies with the temperature, wind velocity and time of the year. The most uncomfortable kind is made of small particles that seem to drive through a person. No clothing can fully protect one from it and it carries a bitter sting as it slings itself against a numb face and collects on the eyelids with intent to freeze there, quite unlike the kind we dream about. This dream-snow is usually viewed by one sitting before a glowing fire, while past the shining window panes floating soft flakes come down, clothing the bare winter world until simple, common objects look like pictures on a Christmas card. In between these two is just ordinary snow. It falls in small flakes and lies there waiting for the wind to pile it into drifts and harden for the youngsters to sleighride on.

Around home we were always competing with the first snow-fall. There was the threshing to finish, vegetables to dig and put away for the winter, range cattle to round up and calves to wean. So many things to do before we could sit back and confine ourselves to winter quarters. We looked for the first snow about the last of October and it generally came with the north wind for an escort, followed by freezing weather. In warm climates, not knowing how lucky they are, people long for ice and snow and tire of their priceless warmth. When a storm came howling across the prairie in winter, it meant hardship and isolation for days or weeks on end. It drove the snow in whirls of blinding white that buried roads and covered fences. In lonely farm houses people were completely cut off from the outside world.

It is surprising how close to nature one can live. If we listen, every living thing has a message of its own. The wind was our weather bureau for, whatever direction it came from, it meant something different in weather. The north wind was responsible for our worst storms and blizzards in winter; in summer, the south and southeast winds were equally dreaded, for a persistent, long drought followed. I loved it best in the spring when the battle of winter was over and everything took on new life. When the saskatoons and high-bush cranberries and chokecherries were in full bloom, we could tell then where the best berries would be later on, and the different kinds. When berry-picking time came we didn't have to waste time looking for patches, for we knew exactly where to go.

The moon and stars were our road-map and the North Star was our principal guide at night. We had to navigate on the prairie the same as on the ocean; it was just as easy to get lost. Incidentally, we took special notice where the crows and hawks built their nests, for these marauders were a constant threat to our chickens. We tried our best to exterminate them, or as many as we could, before they hatched. The jackrabbit changes to winter-white early, if the season calls for it, and the geese and ducks, with an instinct that is always right, will begin their flight southward or delay it according to the season. Papa would go out at night and look at the sky and the different cloud formations and from that, together with the direction of the wind, he could prophesy what the weather would be like the next day, and he didn't miss it very often.

Most of our entertainment in winter centered around house-parties. We did not need much of an excuse to get up a party of some kind. If we couldn't think of a legitimate excuse for some particular kind, there was always the surprise party to fall back on; these were sometimes the most fun. Everyone brought something to eat and the musicians brought their instruments, either violin, guitar or accordion, depending on who came; nearly everyone could play some kind of instrument or help chord on the organ. We were all subject to invasion at any time and especially those who did not feel that they had adequate homes to entertain a crowd by invitation.

I remember so well the first dance that I was allowed to attend; this was at Olaf Walhovd's place. He had built a real nice lumber house and, although he was still single like most of the young homesteaders, he must have had matrimony in the back of his mind when he planned it. It was far from finished inside but the neighbors kept after him to put on a housewarming, so he invited us all to come. This time I got to go along with my two sisters, who happened to be home at the time. I was only twelve years old but being tall for my age I looked much older. Altogether, there were only five girls at this party. Besides the three of us, there were Hannah Vickre and Minnie Hansen. There were nine young men on hand: Ed and Fred Andrew, who furnished the music with their two violins, Olaf and Ole Walhovd, Louie Larsen, Andy Ranneseth, Ole Garstad, Hans Strand and Emil Vallin. As soon as the Andrew boys got their violins tuned up, the dance started and Emil was the first to pick on me. When he discovered that I couldn't dance, he was real disappointed and expressed himself to that effect. Before we had circled the floor, he stopped and looked at me and exclaimed, "Why you can't dance at all!" That hurt, and even though I knew it to be the truth, I retaliated by saying, "And you don't seem to be teaching me very fast."

I'm afraid that was the end of that possible romance; however, in spite of the awkward beginning, I really had a fine time that night. I danced every dance, thanks to the scarcity of girls present. Those boys could really swing one around; every one of them was an excellent dancer and I could not help learning with so many good teachers eager to show me. From then on I attended most of the parties. Dancing was our principal entertainment and how we loved it, especially the waltz, which was my favorite dance. As a beginner, I was cautioned to learn it first before attempting the most intricate steps such as three, four and seven step, polka, Spanish Waltz and French minuet, to name a few. Square dancing was in its heyday, then. We learned dozens of different calls and at most dances every fourth one was a square. The style then was to glide along in a much more refined manner than that of the present, although just as thrilling and exciting, I am sure.

As the land was gradually being settled, we found that we had a community of many different nationalities. People came from all parts of the world, many of whom could not speak the language, but each one had something to contribute. We were all encouraged to hold on to the old traditions and culture from our homeland. We were strangers in a strange country, determined to get ahead on our own and get along with each other; that is what makes a country strong. Canada has a wealth of traditions, brought in by pioneers from older lands. This has culminated in a gracious atmosphere, different from any other place I know; free and easy and friendly towards all, yet dignified.

Whenever a stranger would come looking for a homestead, Papa always took time off and helped whoever it was to find land and pick out the best available quarter section. The Land Office supplied maps, called township maps, that showed what land was still open for filing. The requirements for one to gain title to a homestead included the initial filing fee of ten dollars, six months' residence on the place each year for three years, and to have thirty acres of land plowed for crop. One automatically became a citizen of the country when he completed these requirements and got title.

We were anxious to have families with children settle near us. It was the only way we could ever hope to get a school; besides, we needed some playmates. Nearly all landseekers turned out to be single men, most of whom were good neighbors but poor housekeepers and could always be depended upon to come around about mealtime. They were welcome to share what we had and in fact some of them turned out to be such regulars that we regarded them as belonging, in a kind of way. Every Sunday and holiday we could look for them. If they happened to miss mealtime, there was always coffee and lunch; we always made sure that they had an invitation for Christmas. This is one time a person should not have to spend alone, for thoughts drift back to happier times and bring forth memories that tend to make one homesick when compared with the drab surroundings of a bachelor's shack.

I feel sure they appreciated the hospitality, though very few expressed it in words. Sometimes, one would bring us kids some candy or raisins, if they happened to have some. Most of them were interesting fellows and great readers; they were always bringing books to exchange. Reading was everybody's pastime and hobby; this was before radio or television was invented. Even the ordinary deck of cards provided a great deal of amusement for the man who lived alone; he could entertain himself by the hour playing solitaire. I have often wondered why more of them did not get married. Perhaps it was because they were striving so hard to get ahead financially before asking a girl to share their lot, and this took quite a long time for some, that after a certain length of time they lost their nerve and just kept on dreaming. Each was the kind of man who would really appreciate a good wife.

There were also some peculiar characters among them, too; John Burgh happened to be one of these. According to him, in the country from where he came, the custom was to barter for a wife. He had his eyes on my sisters and offered Papa the best horse he had in trade for either one of them. The girls were furious and refused to speak to him. Papa loved a joke and told John that he better wait until I grew up. John took it seriously and every six months or so he came for a visit, presumably to see how much I had grown. Each time Papa would joke with him and tell him he had to have a better house before he could expect to get married, or a new stove; anything he happened to think of at the time. When I was thirteen he must have thought he had waited long enough. He stopped by our place on his way home from town one day with six hundred pounds of flour and a brand new cook stove in the wagon. When he came in the house, he looked straight at me and said, "You can come now." Mama put a stop to this foolishness once and for all right then and poor John hit the trail as fast as he could, with his cookstove and all.

One day in early April of 1913, we saw a team of white horses hitched to a wagon coming over the hill heading toward our place. We could tell by the kind of load he had that he was a homesteader. He pulled up in the yard and asked if he could camp with us for the night. As soon as he opened his mouth to talk, we knew he was a Swede. His name, he said, was Nels Johnson and when he found that we were Norwegian he knew he was welcome and there was no more English spoken from then on that night. His homestead was one mile east of us; he was married and would send for his wife Ellen as soon as he could get a shack built. In about a month, he went for her and she was a grand person. We kids got scolded for going over there so often. Every Sunday we pretended to be out hunting for crow eggs but instead we circled around and landed up at Johnsons, playing whist. They would beg us to come, not that we needed much coaxing. We got so we could speak Swedish with a real skoning accent. This we had to keep a secret at home, for the folks were so intent on us learning perfect English and that accent is difficult to overcome once you acquire it, same as the Minnesota Norwegian one.

On one of our Sunday scouting trips we found a goose sitting in an old hawk's nest up in a willow tree. Martin braved the attack of the old gander and was surprised to find four great big eggs. We knew Ellen had a setting hen, so we brought the eggs to her and she put them under the hen. This same hen played out on the job after the usual time for hatching chicks expired and another took over. After waiting thirty-six days, we heard some peeping. This continued all day and that night I helped Ellen crack the eggs and out came three Canada goslings; the fourth gave up too soon and had died in the shell. It turned out to be two ganders and one goose; we named them Nels, Ellen and Mr. Young, after another neighbor, an old fellow who claimed to have hunted buffalo with Buffalo Bill on the great plains. The goslings got very tame after we clipped one of their wings to keep them from flying away when a big flock of geese flew over. They were real decoys for as soon as they started honking the flock would break formation and start circling around and come down for a visit with our geese. The wild ones seemed to sense that they were safe. The folks would not allow any hunting whatever on our place and I don't remember eating any wild goose after that.

This same year my sister Martha arrived from the States with her husband, Sam Carlson. Sam filed on a homestead next to ours. Wendel Carlson, Hugh Creed, Billie Collins, Joe Bodis and Jack McGill came in about the same time. Arthur and Walter Wraight had been there for some time and all of these but one were single men. Soon afterwards, the Cy Hubbard family with their five children and Mr. and Mrs. Dave Lyons with their three girls arrived. Right away there was talk of the necessity for a school. Negotiations with the Department of Education in Edmonton began in earnest. The building of Avonlea School was completed in the fall of 1913 and I believe it was the first country school anywhere around. Fred Davis, one of the young bachelors, vowed he would marry the first schoolmarm who taught there and that he did. We had attended school only a very short while when the teacher decided to put on an entertainment. We were scared stiff and hardly any of us could carry a tune but, at any rate, it was a huge success judging by the continuous belly laughter from the audience. There certainly must have been something unusual about our performance because every time someone mentioned the Avonlea School concert, they would shake their heads and start laughing again.

Martha and Sam built their house a short distance down the hill from us. When Agnes, their first baby, was born she was the object of our affection. Soon Ellen and Nels announced that they expected a baby too; we could hardly wait for the event to happen. Finally one evening in December, Nels pounded on our door. We could tell that something unusual was in the air for he talked Swedish at a runaway gait, asking Mama to hurry and come right away. Papa hitched the team to the bobsleigh and cautioned us kids to be real careful with the fire. He filled the heating stove full of coal and promised to be back before midnight. After a while we began to feel hungry and decided to make some cocoa. I put the big kettle on the stove, filled it half full of milk, added a goodly amount of sugar and half of the cocoa in the box. We were really having a party and enjoying ourselves when I happened to notice the stove. It was pure white from heat and so was the stovepipe, right up to the ceiling. I grabbed a bucket and ran outside, scooped it full of snow and poured it in the stove, then another; needless to say, it cooled things off, though we had water all over the floor. It was a wonder the stove didn't crack. Then the six cups of cocoa we each had consumed began to take effect. Ole and I got sick and neither of us could ever relish cocoa again after that. Martin finished what was left in the pot and never batted an eye. When Papa came home, he told us that Ellen had a little baby girl and I could hardly wait to see her. They named her Ruth. I had been Ellen's girl for a long time and wondered if she would need me now since she had a baby of her own. I felt quite relieved when she assured me that I would always be her big girl and I continued to be until she died, although she had three of her own by then.

Chapter VII

To keep on breaking up sod, one must have sharp plowshares and for this a blacksmith shop of some kind is necessary. We managed during the first couple of years with an open fireplace outside, and a piece of railroad iron for an anvil and a small bellows that we had to keep pumping constantly to keep the coals hot. We learned to gauge the heat of the iron when it was time to pull the share and start pounding it. This was not one of our favorite after-supper pastimes; we took turns at it and were mighty glad there were three of us to change off. We never argued about whose turn it was—we knew.

The bellows was made of a short piece of pipe with some chamois from an old coat lining tacked on to a frame made from an old packing box. It worked fine. While Papa pounded and sharpened one share we had to get the next one ready for him. This kind of primitive blacksmithing would not do forever and as we were tired of building sod houses we agreed to build a shop from rocks. This was one way that we could put them to a useful purpose and at the same time get rid of them. We abandoned the idea however when it was two-thirds finished and turned it into a smokehouse instead. The next year we got some lumber and built a little shop typical of that period on the prairie.

The reason for the smokehouse was that we now had a pig, a huge skinny razorback that Hugh Creed had won in a poker game in Veteran. Hugh got as far as our place with him and offered to take five dollars for him and wait for the money. With good care and feed the pig put on plenty of new meat and grew to such a size by killing time that we had lard, cured and smoked meat enough to last us a whole year.

Then came the rumors of war. Hugh Creed, who was a reservist in the British Army, was first to announce that he was going. He brought us a couple of heavy overcoats that he had no more need for and stayed for supper. We were sad to see him leave; he joined the Princess Pat Regiment from Calgary. One by one the boys followed. There were farewell parties, basket socials and dances every week for some volunteer. Many hundreds of dollars went to Red Cross from the proceeds.

Wendel Carlson bought a lovely white pony with saddle. I borrowed him so often that he decided he might just as well sell him to me and get himself another. I loved that horse; he was a real cow pony and as easy to ride as a rocking horse. He had a peculiar little dog-trot gait that was unique. I kept him tied in the barn at all times, for he was impossible to catch if turned loose. When we tried to rope him on the run, he would stop short, hold his nose to the ground until the lariat loop would slide right off him, then he was on the dead run again. That was the reason he was always under the saddle. We rode wherever we went; rounding up the cattle, visiting neighbors or to town for the mail.

The pleasure that I got out of riding is hard to describe. When we were roaming over the prairie I used to lean over and whisper in his ear, which he seemed to understand perfectly and would pick up his ears and point them forward. At other times he would flatten them right back as if he did not quite agree. Always when I pulled the cinch a little too tight, he would nip at my sleeve as if to say, "That's enough now." I used to practise picking up a handkerchief off the ground while he was on a dead run which he seemed to enjoy as much as I did and knew how close to come to it without being guided. Billy was my constant companion for many years. Later on, I have a real story to tell about Billy Boy.

We got used to all kinds of queer characters stopping by our place. Once, when one such happened to be a woman, we could hardly believe our own eyes, for she swung off her horse in real cowboy fashion and greeted us with a "Howdy, folks." It was easy to see that she was wise to the ways of the range. She dropped the bridle reins on the ground and left her horse; he stood as if he were tied. A horse had to be whipbroke to be trained like that. It takes an expert horseman to do it, too. She claimed that she was out looking for her horses; her brand was the Box P and she introduced herself as Mamy Purtee. She was a big, husky woman with white hair and a leather-beaten look in her face.

Mama asked her to sit down and have a cup of coffee. We were real fond of potato cakes, which are somewhat like pancakes only made with boiled potatoes and best eaten cold. Whenever we got hungry between meals, we would run in and grab a couple, spread with butter and brown sugar, and when rolled up they tasted mighty good. We did not consider them company fare; however, Mama hadn't had time to put them away before our guest spied them. "What are those things?" she inquired. After Mama had explained, she decided that she would try anything once and proceeded to make them disappear. All of a sudden, she took one look at me, gulped and swallowed a couple times and blurted out, "I'll bet you can ride like an Indian!" I almost fell backward, and began to look for some excuse to get away. Mama told her that I could ride as well as any boy, Indian or white. She was determined to take me home with her for a visit to help her round up her horses. I didn't know what Mama would say to that, so I sneaked outside and was not to be found. She came back several times and we never did find out what she really wanted, since her horses did not graze in our part of the country. She may have meant well enough but I had the most peculiar feeling about her, and whenever I saw her heading in our direction, I jumped on my pony and rode around until she was out of sight.

One evening a horse trader landed in at our place, bent on trading a saddlehorse which he claimed was a real good one. We had a cow that was so hard to milk that only Papa could manage to get any milk from her. He was not fond of milking and had been looking for some excuse to get rid of her for some time, and now was his chance. It is not often that both parties in a trade get cheated, but that is exactly what happened in this instance. They traded even; he took our cow and left his horse. When we tried her out next morning, she turned out to be a big disappointment to us, being slower than the oxen. The only kick we got out of her was to pinch her back in a certain place. She would then rear up and throw herself backward on the ground. We tried to see which one could stay on the longest before she fell. This was quite amusing and somehow we managed to get off just in time.

Chapter VIII

We were watching with interest the railroad extending east toward us. Every time we went to Wheatbelt Store we would look for some sign of activity where the townsite was laid out. The name of the town was Veteran and Bob Wilson informed us that he was building a large general store and intended to move his business to town as soon as it was finished. This was to be a two storey building, with the upstairs to be used as a Community Hall. The first time we drove in just to satisfy our curiosity there were piles of lumber here and there with several crews of carpenters hammering away at what turned out to be The Bank of Toronto, the Crown Lumber Yard, Erickson's Livery Barn, as well as Judy's Restaurant and Kenney McKinsey's Blacksmith Shop. These were the first buildings in town, along with Wilson's Store.

The Home Restaurant could also be counted as among the first, for very soon my sisters, Sina and Lillie, decided to start a business of their own and built this restaurant. Many an oldtimer, I am sure, will remember buying a meal ticket for six dollars, which enabled him to eat three meals a day for six days; or supper, bed and breakfast for one dollar. It is unbelievable in these times to think of getting a night's lodging and two meals for just one dollar. My sisters were resourceful girls and without their aid we would have had a hard time on the homestead. Whenever the need arose for new shoes, clothes or machinery, it was the girls we depended upon. There were no handouts in the form of relief in those days and I doubt if my family would have accepted such, if it had been available.

The C.P.R. depot served also as a makeshift church at first. We used to attend Sunday School as well as church service in the waiting room until Wilson's Hall was completed. After that the Hall was the center of all activities, even serving as a school for the ten grades of children until a school could be built. The United Farmers of Alberta made their headquarters here, too, and I used to enjoy listening to their meetings which were conducted strictly according to parliamentary rules.

Friday night was dance night and the one night we looked forward to each week. We had variety in our dances in those days. The type depended largely upon the season and time of year, such as the New Year's dance, St. Valentine's or St. Patrick's and the ever-popular masquerade dance. I remember one such dance when Johnny Molohon walked off with first prize as Tom Sawyer. Everyone there marvelled at the little white dog that followed right at his heels all evening, never leaving him for a minute, even when he was dancing. We did not discover until the dance was over the secret for the dog's continued faithfulness to John, when he asked for a pair of scissors to cut loose the string from a big, raw beefsteak which he had wrapped around his leg.

July first was the big day to which we all looked forward. Everyone came from far and near, in wagons, buggies and on horseback, to celebrate Dominion Day. The first celebration seemed to have made the greatest impression on me, most especially the parade. The different business establishments advertised in the most unique manner. Mike LaBarge, the local butcher, had a display of freshly-killed gophers hanging in neat rows on his meat wagon. Then there was a single ox hitched to an old model T Ford, to represent transportation. Two young men clowned and cut capers as a circus mule and many others, the most outstanding being Charlie Inman as Chief of his tribe, with the Neutral Hill boys decked out in war paint and feathers, to represent real Indians. Mr. Inman was proud of the fact that he was part Indian. He was a leader in sports, especially baseball. He organized the Big Four Baseball League and acted as manager for a number of years. The teams, representing their various communities, were Neutral Valley, Lakesend, Talbot and Silver Heights.

The baseball game in the afternoon was the highlight of the day and caused as much excitement as any big league game could. There were usually three teams to compete for the prize. They drew lots to see which two played first and the team that got the bye in the draw felt pretty lucky. Nose Hill and Talbot often picked the best players from both teams to try and beat the town boys, which they often did.

Frank Slough was the official umpire for all games. Every team seemed to abide by his decision without the usual disagreements. He was a fine gentleman as well as a good sport. Alec and Jack Martin, Doc Ballentyne and Staples were some of the Veteran ball players of that time.

The climax came in the evening when the lights were turned on in the Wilson Hall and the musicians started to tune up their instruments. The McGowan Orchestra was something special to listen to, as well as dance to. With young and old, little and big, the huge Hall was soon filled and the fun began. The only intermission was for the midnight lunch. We had to watch the clock and get back to the Restaurant to help prepare for the crowd. As soon as lunch was over, we all went back to the Hall and danced until the sun came peeping over the rim of the horizon.

Things got pretty lively at times toward the end. The Bar-O-Five boys could generally be depended upon to lend a little gaiety and invent a few pranks before leaving town. On one such occasion, I remember, they got an old sorrel horse and painted it with stripes to represent a zebra. They then dared George Rolls to ride it into the Bank of Toronto to get a check cashed. Whether George succeeded in getting the money from Mr. Staples I cannot say.

Veteran was a real cow town in that everybody had a cow, including us at the restaurant. The town water pump was located right in the center of Main street and everybody carried water in pails from this well; in addition, there was a water trough on the side for the horses and cows to drink from. People hadn't had time to dig wells, as yet, on their own.

One after the other, the grain elevators were built and the trek of grain haulers got to be a common sight. Some of the farmers lived more than twenty miles away and could only make one trip every two days. In good years, from the time threshing got underway in the fall until late spring, they kept on hauling grain. Both horses and men took a beating when the thermometer began to drop to twenty below zero and on down. No teamster could afford to trot his team, either loaded or empty, for fear they would get too warm, then freeze and catch cold. At the same time, the driver could not stand to sit on the wagon for any length of time, so had to walk most of the way to keep warm.

Herb Scott was one of our colorful early settlers. He lived about twenty miles north of town on the Ribstone Creek and drove mules, which in itself was an oddity. We could look for his string of six mules hitched to the grain tank loaded with wheat to roll in about dusk; he left home before daylight in the morning, spending all day on the trail. He stayed at the restaurant overnight like many other grain haulers and started for home right after breakfast the next morning for another load.

Chapter IX

In the fall of 1914 we were busy threshing wheat when a livery team with two men in a buggy drove up to see one of the men on the outfit. I was delegated, against my will, that day to drive the oxen hitched to the grain wagon, back and forth from the threshing outfit to the granary. My Dad did all the shovelling; all I had to do was drive the empty wagon back to the machine then take the full load to the granary. It was real chilly weather and Mama insisted on me wearing boys' pants at that time, so I was the object of much teasing and comments from the crew. Our boys were needed to keep the straw away from the straw-carrier and I couldn't think up a single excuse not to do it, much as I hated to display my skill in front of all those men.

Just as I pulled up to the grain spout and finally got the wagon spotted by much pulling and hauling on the reins, shouting and prodding each ox in turn with some help from the stick, I looked up to see the best-looking young fellow standing there, laughing his head off. "Well," he said, "you're some skinner. What is your name?" "Ranghild Olsen," I answered politely. "What?" he asked, and when I repeated it he was away on another spree. By now I both looked and felt like a cooked lobster and I know if anyone had dared tell me then that this young man was to be my future husband, I would have told him to go stick his head in a gopher hole. I felt hurt and angry, still I could not get him off my mind. I had no idea who he was, or where he came from.

The next time I saw him was in Veteran. He brought a carload of young people from Coronation to a dance. Crowds of people came from all around, most of them in time for supper at the restaurant. A room was engaged for the ladies to dress in for the dance. This meant a lot of extra work for the girls, so our whole family turned to and helped in whatever way we could.

I was delighted to take in the cash at the counter that night, when Roy walked in. He came right over to me with a wide grin and said, "remember me?" I didn't know what to say, for I really wanted to forget about ever having driven an ox right then, let alone talk about it. He kept on, "I just can't remember that name of yours. Could you tell me once more?" I'm afraid I was a bit sarcastic for I felt sure he was making fun of me, so I said, "If your memory is that bad, why bother." He looked somewhat hurt, then turned around and said, "Anyway, you've got the most beautiful hair I have ever seen." That helped to break down the barrier somewhat. He then told me teasingly that he would love to take me to the dance. That, I didn't believe. He was most interesting and before long he told me his name was Roy Merriken; that he came from Maryland and had a homestead in Nose Hills; also, that he wanted more than anything to learn to dance. It did not take Roy very long to learn to dance. Almost before I realized it, he was the best dancer around, in my estimation at least.

He also had more girl friends than you could shake a stick at but I was not one of them, however, being too young, as well as quite independent. He was a regular visitor at our place for many years before I had the slightest idea that he was the least bit interested in me. He used to tease me unmercifully and cuff me around, calling me such nicknames as Slim, Skinny, besides the regular Shorty. He took my sister to dances quite often and always insisted that I go along. We danced together a great deal and I looked forward to these dances with genuine pleasure.

Coming home from town we did not always follow the same wagon trail we first made. If the sun were high and we were making good time, we often detoured and cut across country to see if we could locate any new neighbors. We had heard that a homesteader was digging in three miles south of us. We were curious to meet him and on this particular day we headed off in that direction to see if it was so and what kind of a fellow he was.

It is difficult to find a dugout in a sidehill on one hundred and sixty acres, especially when the land is as hilly and rolling as it happens to be south of our place. We hunted around for quite a while and were about to give up when we noticed some smoke coming out of the ground some distance away. We drove close enough to see a mound of dirt with a stovepipe sticking out of it. Papa went over to investigate and, sure enough, there was a man digging and carrying dirt out of a hole in the ground, but this was no ordinary man.

When Papa greeted him in the usual frontier manner, he just stood there and stared; all of a sudden, he let go with a squeal that would do credit to a mountain lion, while pointing in every direction. It was only when he pulled a small scratch pad from his pocket and began to scribble away that it dawned on us that he must be deaf and dumb. When he finished writing, he emphasized every word with more squealing. It was a bit frightening for he was a powerful man about fifty and rather savage looking. He had filed on this homestead and was digging in for the winter, he wrote. Most dugouts that I have seen are in a sidehill, however, Dummy, as we called him, went straight down like a badger and dug a straight hole placing poplar poles with hay and dirt on top for a roof; he had to climb a ladder through a trap-door in the roof to get outside. He got to be a big nuisance before long, trying to attract attention with his piercing shrieks if he thought we were not paying enough attention to what he wanted to tell us.

All homesteaders were most careful with matches. It was an unwritten law on the prairie never to toss a match away. All pipe smokers had some kind of lid on their pipes to keep sparks from flying. Dummy did not adhere to any such law and it was through his carelessness that we experienced the worst prairie fire in our part of the country.

One day in the summer of 1914 while Dummy was walking home from town, he lit his pipe and threw the match on the ground. The match ignited the prairie grass and before long it had gotten such a start that it was beyond control. Dummy first noticed it when he smelled the smoke, for he could not hear the hiss and crackle of the fire behind him. When he looked back and saw what he had done, he ran as fast as he could to the nearest house, screeching in his peculiar manner, pointing to the fire. It did not take long before every man within sight of the smoke knew of the danger. Some started plowing additional fire guards; others backfired and still others fought with wet sacks. Some tried to protect the buildings and haystacks in the path of the fire by plowing two strips and firing in between; it was coming toward us like a blazing inferno. Four plow teams, one behind the other, were heading north trying to protect the grain fields to the west. We kids rounded up what cattle we could see and pushed them out of the danger zone. One by one the haystacks went up in flames; all our grazing land was burnt to a crisp; the dry willow around the sloughs added fuel to the fire and made it roar like a blast furnace. What was worse, there went our dry wood which we depended on for the cookstove and kindling.

When Papa came home we could hardly recognize him for his eyes were bloodshot, eyebrows and hair singed, face as red as fire and his clothes as black as soot. Dummy was a scared man for a while. When he did pick up enough nerve to go to town, the boys hauled him into court, had a mock trial and sentenced him; no more smoking under any circumstances or go to jail. This he adhered to as long as he stayed in the community.

As a youngster I had a particular fondness for cats. They have a peculiar instinct, a keen sense of knowing who likes them and who doesn't.

One that I was real fond of was Old Puss, a big, black tomcat. As long as I stayed home, he wouldn't leave the place. If I happened to go away for any length of time, he moved up to the Johnson's and made himself at home there and seemed perfectly contented. As soon as I was back home, here came Puss, just as if someone had told him. It puzzled all of us and we wondered how he could sense it from a mile away. When I got married, neither of us was superstitious so I brought my cat with me and he lived to the ripe old age of twenty-one.

Another unique specimen was Anna, a lovely white Persian. When we moved to town we left her on the farm and she immediately went on a hunger strike. Linde, our hired man, phoned us to come and get the blamed cat before she starved to death. When we left for the States, she again refused to eat, and this time she died. She lasted two weeks after we had gone, going from one room to another all day looking for us. She finally got so weak that she couldn't stand, still refusing any food set before her.

When we first opened the restaurant in Veteran, an old mom cat with six kittens took up residence outside the kitchen door. Every time the door opened she tried to sneak in. The girls tried every way they knew how to get rid of her but nobody wanted a black cat family and no one would shoot her. Lillie offered me a dollar to shoot her. I thought about it for several days before I decided to go through with it. I made a perfect shot with a twenty-two rifle; she didn't even move. I gave Florence Boone, a young school girl, ten cents to take her out in the country and bury her. It was easy money earned. However, I did not feel very gallant about that transaction and often wished I hadn't done it. It's the only cat I ever killed.

One fall when our cats had been real prolific, I had thirteen black kittens and every one followed me wherever I went around the farm. One day, as I was on my down to see Martha, I met a team and buggy with two men from town, bent on a hunting expedition. Meeting thirteen black cats was too much for Mr. Bidleman, who at best was a superstitious fellow. He stopped suddenly, wheeled the horses around and beat it back to town. I will never forget the expressions he used in relation to black cats spoiling his hunting trip.

A few days later the same two hunters came by and we heard two shots in rapid succession just south of the house in the slough where our geese had the habit of swimming. We ran as fast as we could to see and there lay Nels and Mr. Young, floating and dead. The hunters, now realizing what they had done, got away as fast as they could. It was a sad day for us. We buried the ganders and Ellen walked around honking and honking; it was easy to see that she was a lonesome goose. We decided to let her wing grow so that she could fly away if she wanted to. She stayed with us until one day late in the fall when a flock of geese coaxed her along on their flight south. The next spring, as I watched a big flock of geese winging their way north, one lone goose left the formation and settled down in our yard. It was Ellen, for sure. She stood for a moment, her neck outstretched, glup-glupping at me. Then, all of a sudden, she flew back and joined the rest. That was the last time we saw her.

Teenage, or the awkward age, as it was called when I grew up, is a difficult time for every youngster. This is when youth needs love and guidance more than any other thing. We went through frustrations same as the teenager of today, only we were disciplined to a far greater extent. Our parents' order was law and we were taught to have great respect for the older generation and their opinions. This was a good thing; somehow, down through the years, this lesson has been side-tracked and lost. No matter who you are or where you go, one must have something to work for, cling to or be guided by. Even the most experienced sea captain, who knows the waters of the bay or inlet by heart, looks for the light in the lighthouse by night or the buoys by day to guide his ship in the right channel, past the treacherous places and safely into harbor; otherwise, his ship might go on the rocks. A human is not much different. We were fortunate in that we were included in all activities with the grown people and made to feel important and that we really belonged.

When I was fifteen, I ushered a baby into the world. This baby happened to be my nephew, Marvin LaBarge. I was to stay with my sister, Sina, while her husband went after the doctor, who, unfortunately, was away. Mike then drove as fast as he could to get Mama. Delivering babies was nothing new to her for she was a licensed baby doctor in Norway. She did not however have a license to practise in Canada, so only in emergencies did she help out and was glad for the opportunity to be of help at a critical time.

Sina lived in town, which was nine miles from the homestead. Mike had a crack team of standard-bred horses that I'm sure he drove on the dead run, but they still were not fast enough, for when Mama arrived on the scene, it was all over. I don't know for sure which suffered most, Sina or I, and I had my doubts about ever wanting to get married for a long time after that. I loved my sister intensely; it was somewhat of a hero worship that I felt toward her. She was a beautiful girl with big brown eyes and dark hair, which was my idea of real beauty, and I often wished that I looked like her. When I was real tiny, I used to dream that I had changed to look like her. What a disappointment I felt upon jumping out of bed, running to the mirror to find out for sure, only to find there staring back at me were the same green eyes and the same red hair.

It is surprising how the pioneer women managed. Mrs. Watson, one of our neighbors, was all alone when she took sick. She gathered the baby clothes under her arm and walked to her friend and neighbor, Mrs. Lyons. She got there in the nick of time for Mrs. Lyons to deliver a fine boy. Mother and son stayed on for a ten-day visit, receiving the best of care.

Chapter X

This land was being taken up rapidly. One of the last to homestead was Berglund who located with Papa's help about two and a half miles southeast of us. He built a little shack, then brought his wife down from Iron Creek where she was staying with her folks. He came from Sweden; she from Norway; neither one could speak English to amount to anything. She was a lovely person and we all thought a great deal of her.

One day, a hunter came into the restaurant and told us that he had stopped at a place where there was a very sick lady. When he described the place, we knew who it was, so the girls hired a livery team and sent for her to be brought to town. They fixed up a room for her and I waited on her the best I could. We were so busy that I couldn't find much time to devote to her but I did manage to bring her fresh water occasionally and whatever she asked for, which was very little. Doctor Day, who I believe was the first doctor we had in Veteran, was boarding with us at the time. He did what he could to ease her pain but he soon decided that she had to have an operation.

Cris Gaardsmoen, another boarder, built a stretcher and with the help of the train crew on the C.P.R., took her into the baggage car on the train and helped get her to the Consort Hospital. Just before she left, she thanked all of us. She gave me her Bible for being so good to wait on her; she said that was all she had. She died shortly after the operation and when it came time to arrange for the funeral there was no money to buy a coffin. She would have been buried in a rough box had it not been for Dr. Day, who ordered a nice coffin and gave her a decent burial. I heard him say that if he never received a cent in return, it was money well spent for she was too lovely a lady to be put away in a rough box. The husband finally got word to her relatives and when they did come, they asked for the Bible which I gave to them without any explanation. They reimbursed Dr. Day for the hospital and funeral expenses but I still think he deserved a great deal of credit for doing what he did.

In 1916 the people of Nose Hill community organized and built a school. There were not enough children in a single district four by five miles to procure permission from the Department of Education for a school, therefore it was decided to make it a consolidated by taking in another district. The school house was built on the line between the two. There was considerable controversy about the location at first. It took several meetings to decide where. These meetings were held at Bob Gray's place and even though he was a bachelor he settled the matter by donating an acre of land in the corner of his homestead for the site. Taxes were a big issue. The majority of taxpayers were single men who no doubt had hopes, even though they had no immediate prospects of getting any benefits from a school. However, they voted for it with the understanding that it would be used for entertainment purposes as well and had a clause inserted in the petition to that effect. This has been carried out diligently through the years.

On Sunday we looked forward to the baseball game at Nose Hills. Since most of us rode horseback there were just about as many horses as people present. The Bar-O-Five and the Nose Hills teams were evenly matched. When either or both teams were short of players, which was quite often the case, they would choose players from the crowd and the game was on. At one time, our minister umpired the game and after it was over we all went to church in the schoolhouse.

On one particular Sunday a man came out from town in his new model T Ford to watch the game. As it happened, Ben Molohon brought Ida Hubbard and me to the game that day in a buggy drawn by a crack team of standard-bred horses. They got to arguing about which was the faster mode of travel and decided to settle it by racing the mile from the school house to George Henwood's corner. We girls had no idea what was happening and did not know about the bet until we started for home and they both got lined up and gave a yell. We were off like a shot. Mike pulled the gas lever as far down as it would go, while Ben grabbed the whip and stood up in the front of the buggy and whooped and hollered. There was only a wagon trail in which the ruts were deep and the car had the right-of-way to start with, so we took to the side of the road. The horses ran like mad and Ida and I were holding on for dear life. We must have hit at least a hundred badger holes and bumps; at times it felt like we left the earth. We won the race but at this point the horses were running away. They circled around a quarter section of land for fully fifteen minutes before quieting down enough to get control of them. Ben must have collected the bet, for he bought each of us a box of candy the next Sunday.

From then on life was one great adventure. Just to be young with the whole world before you is wonderful in itself. We did not have the many advantages that young people have today, yet I believe we got more enjoyment out of life by having to create our own amusements.

We didn't mind going ten or fifteen miles to a dance in below-zero weather, with a good team of horses jogging along to the tune of sleigh-bells, and all tucked in with robes, blankets and a footwarmer to keep our feet from freezing. We could always manage to keep our hands warm regardless of how cold it got. Human nature does not change and it was as popular to hold hands then as it is now, and always will be.

We could see the lights in the Nose Hill School for several miles and as we came closer we could often see that the dance was already in full swing with the couples dancing past the windows, one by one. When we got close enough to hear the music, if we listened intently we could tell whether Harold Wilson or Earl Beebe was playing the violin to start things off or if John Ekrol had gotten there. Yes, it was most often John with Mrs. Witt on the piano and Henry Davis on the drums. We hurried so that we would not lose a minute. While the horses were unhitched, blanketed and put in the barn, I carried the cake carefully and put it with a lot of others on the shelf in the girls' cloakroom.

By the time I could get my many wraps off, my partner was waiting and we sailed across the floor in perfect rhythm in anticipation of the grandest time ever. Halfway around the floor, someone would ask you for the next dance and so it went on in a round of enjoyment until midnight. Then the floor manager would call out "Partners for the sup-per waltz." No girl ever had to eat by herself as there were many more men than girls. Most often, we bunched together in groups with the extra men included and all shared in the fun.

Annie Beebe was the official coffee maker for years. She brought drinking water from home in two five gallon cream cans to make it with. When it came time to put the copper washboiler on the little camp stove to make coffee, she took a look at the crowd first to see how much to make. She would either add more or dip out some water according to the number of people present and Annie always seemed to hit it right. The admission charge was one dollar for the men; the ladies brought cake.

Chapter XI

I happened to be in Coronation getting some dental work done when I received a phone call from Dr. Little saying that I better come home right away because my mother was very ill and he thought she would die before morning. This was in the evening and there was absolutely no way for me to get home except by train and that did not leave until next morning. I walked the floor all night. Papa was waiting for me at the depot when I arrived in Veteran and we hurried as fast as we could but Mama passed away a short while after we got home. We were a grief-stricken family. Only one month before we had lost our lovely sister, Sina, and now Mama had left us too. We hardly knew what to do; no one came to help, for the neighbors did not seem to realize what had happened. Between us, we managed to dress and lay her out in the coffin. The nearest cemetery was twenty-five miles away and as this was early spring the roads were almost impassable. Papa went to town on a Sunday and he had to wait until the next day to get into the stores but we worried for fear he had met with an accident. Where before we had been carefree, even careless, we now got that awful feeling that when misfortune strikes twice, it generally lurks around the corner for a third attack.

The Likness family were old friends of the folks from Norway. They lived at Monitor, about thirty-five miles southeast from our place. They had a large family and the two youngest children, Selmer and Julia, were about my own age. I was invited to spend some time at their place and was glad of the opportunity to get away for a while. The Shannons were close neighbors of theirs; they farmed a lot of land and had a big herd of cattle. The crop was poor this year and Mr. Shannon was looking for someone to herd his cattle on the fields; this was herd-law country with no fences anywhere. He had heard that I was used to riding, so he came over one evening and asked if I wanted the job at twenty-five dollars a month for two months or until the cattle were ready for market. This was the average wage for a hired man at that time; girls were only getting about ten.

He had a lot of oats planted and my job would be to keep the cattle on his field and off the neighbor's cropland. I had my pick of three saddlehorses. I tried them all and chose the one that I found best to my liking. Together with Sport, a fine collie dog that belonged to the Likness family but wanted to stay with me, we had a grand time. I really enjoyed that job, especially the two weeks that I was close to the Langakers. Every afternoon Mrs. Langaker, who was the nicest old lady, came out in the yard waving her apron to attract my attention. Then, when I heard the familiar "yoo hoo," I knew I was in for a real treat of Norwegian cookies, coffee and conversation, and it didn't take me long to get over there. I had to drive the cattle home for water every evening and into a pasture; then, after taking care of my horse, I was free to do as I pleased. Mrs. Shannon was a wonderful cook and I thoroughly enjoyed sitting down to a good meal without having to cook it. I stayed the two months but by now Papa and the boys were tired of batching and wanted me to come home. I left the job, taking with me many pleasant memories of the time I spent at Monitor as a regular cowgirl.

We were among the first to catch the Spanish flu in 1918. A couple of cross-country travellers stopped at our place overnight. Before long, first one then another of us took sick; Ole was the first, then Lillie. Papa had gone back to Bawlf with Uncle Knud, who had been visiting us. Martin and I could feel it coming on, so managed to pack in plenty of wood and coal and filled all available buckets with water. I milked the cow, and it took both of us to carry the milk to the house even after pouring out half of it. Our backs were killing us. Ole was delirious and Lillie was burning up with fever, too. About the third day, we were desperate to know what to do. Annie, our cow, stood outside the bedroom window bawling unmercifully, needing to be milked. This didn't help our headaches any. We hadn't seen Sam or Martha for several days and felt sure that they must be sick or else they would have been to see us.

Finally, we remembered the distress signal of the wilderness; three shots in succession. Between us, Martin and I dragged the big forty-sixty Marlin rifle to the east window towards Johnsons, stuck the gun barrel out, resting it on the window ledge, and pointed it upward. We fired the three shots, then waited for about a minute before firing three more. Nels heard it and knew something must be wrong. He had lived in Alaska for several years before coming to Alberta and that was the code they used in the woods up there. He came right away, milked the cow and fed the saddlehorse. He then went on home to bring us some food; this he left outside and talked to us through the window. Martin and I were also real sick by now. The most we could manage to do was to get some water for the other two; to do this we crawled on the floor.

We didn't dare try to go outside to get the food Nels had left but it didn't matter much anyway since none of us could eat anything.

However, we appreciated the gesture and hoped that Papa would come home. When he finally came, he was a busy man for a while. He went to town the same day to get some medicine for us and found Dr. Little, along with half the townspeople, sick. The schoolhouse had been turned into a hospital and was filling up fast. Those who were still able to travel were bringing sick ones in from the country, especially the men who lived alone had to be looked after.

Papa went to the drugstore and asked for a bottle of brandy. We had prohibition at that time but the government allowed plenty for medical purposes. The druggist, scared stiff of the epidemic and wearing a mask, refused to give him any. When Papa pulled off his coat and, with a determined look, said, "We will see whether I get some," Mr. Hogarth was frightened enough to let him have it. We took it by spoonful; this seemed to be the only thing that did us any good. We all pulled through, thanks to a lot of luck, ingenuity and a bottle of brandy.

Chapter XII

One of the really outstanding events of my recollection was the Big Gap Stampede of 1919 at Neutral Hills. The location was ideal. It was situated on the south side of a gradual slope of the sidehill a quarter of a mile long which served as a natural grandstand for the five thousand spectators. People came from far and near in wagons, on horseback or in buggies, for very few had automobiles, as yet. The stampede was highly advertised as a Wild West show; the local cowboys practised for weeks such plays as Sitting Bull on War Path and several others. The people who brought tents were lucky. Some slept in their wagons, while others spread their blankets on the ground, and still others danced all night and kept going. This was a four day affair and each day there was a different program of entertainment. It took a lot of know-how and skill on the part of the cowboys to execute the spills from horseback without getting hurt. There had to be much shooting with blanks and the horses had to get accustomed to it, plus a lot of practising and timing for the different acts of these Indian stories. The battle of Custer's Last Stand looked so real that I was afraid for some of the boys; one of those fighting the Indians was my brother Ole.

Every afternoon there was the bronco and steer riding competitions, wild-cow milking contest and calf roping. Grey Ghost was the champion bucking horse. He was known to be a killer, which made him very famous. We all held our breath when this outlaw started sunfishing, then proceeded to go through every trick known to man or horse to try to get rid of his rider. Frank Gibson was the successful contestant and was proclaimed champion cowboy.

The old-time barbecue pit was a real novelty. The boys dug a big hole and lined it with rocks. A group of them sat up all night burning brush and wood in this until the rocks were red hot, then a large covered roasting pan containing two steers quartered and seasoned with salt and pepper by the pound was lowered into the pit and covered with hot ashes, then dirt. This was left until the next evening, when we all lined up for a chunk of beef with boiled potatoes. Some ate just for the curiousity of it but we all ended up eating more than usual. I know I did, for this was the most delicious barbecued meat that I have ever tasted. When the boys uncovered the huge roaster and opened the lid, the meat was ready to fall off the bones. They used a round pointed shovel to scoop up the meat and place it on a table where it was distributed on a first-come, first-served basis, free of charge. The steers were donated by the Circle J Ranch. There were forty booths or concessions on the grounds and each one seemed busy selling food to the tremendous crowd.

Each afternoon there was a vaudeville performance in the big tent. The main feature was the new song hit, "Till We Meet Again," which was sung by an Indian chief, White Eagle, from the U.S.A. He was a splendid-looking fellow with a fine voice. I went to hear him every day and even now, after all these years, when I hear this song, it reminds me of the stampede and White Eagle.

Long before the sun went down, the dance was in full swing on a huge platform in the open. The men paid ten cents each time they danced. The floor was crowded and stayed that way until three o'clock in the morning or until the musicians finally played out. A Bowery dance has a most romantic atmosphere; soft music with a full moon hanging low in a star-spangled sky; a soft, careless breeze drifting by while you glide along in the arms of your best fellow; these are the memories to cherish.

This was the real old West. Ranching was in its heyday with cowboys on every ranch. I want to emphasize the fact that they were fine fellows and good sports. They did not pack guns and I never knew of anyone to hurt or kill anybody, like the present television audience is supposed to believe. If there happened to be any disagreement or trouble among them, which seldom happened, they fought like gentlemen, with their fists. When the fight was over, that was the end of it.

Twins seem to run in our family for both my mother and grandmother had twins; then Martha surprised us with a little girl and boy, but the girl died at birth. We were unprepared for such a tragedy. However, in traditional frontier fashion, we did the best we could under the circumstances. Dr. Little baptized the baby; Papa built a little coffin which I padded and lined while Sam dug the grave in the corner of the yard. It was a strange funeral; only three of us present. Papa read the twenty-third Psalm and said a prayer. I placed a bunch of wild flowers on the casket and finally Sam planted a little wooden cross which he had made and inscribed to mark the grave. There was no Lutheran Church established near us and our minister lived at Provost, about forty miles away. Pastor Settre did however conduct church service once a month during the summer, at the different members' homes.

One Sunday morning Lillie and I were on our way to church, driving a team of young colts hitched to a buggy. We were making good time when all of a sudden, a huge tumbling mustard rolled toward us. The horses became frightened, took the bits in their mouths and away they went over humps and into holes, bolting sideways and finally breaking the pole. When this happened, we were pulled right out of the buggy to the ground, but we both held on to the reins and were dragged some distance. When the horses finally quieted down and stopped long enough for us to get hold of them, they were wringing wet and shaking all over. We separated them and, after walking around for a while to cool them off some, we climbed on top of the harness and rode back home. Lillie was skinned up some but I escaped without a scratch. The next day we went back and picked up the wreckage.

Chapter XIII

I was nineteen when I decided to get a business education and set out for Calgary to enrol for a term at the Garbutt Business College. I soon realized what money I had would not cover room and board, plus tuition, for very long. The college had a list of applications from good homes all over the city asking for girls to help with housework in exchange for their keep. This I took advantage of and was assigned to a nice family by the name of Sparling in Elbow Park. I walked the fourteen blocks to school every night and morning and carried my lunch. Mrs. Sparling set a formal table, so I always knew there would be the same huge pile of dishes waiting for me. My main duty otherwise was to care for two small boys every night except Sunday when I insisted on going to church. This gave me a lot of time for study and my progress was quite satisfactory.

I loved the city of Calgary and intended to stay on after graduation. It was the custom of the college to help secure a job for the graduate and this they did. I wanted to go home to see the folks before I took a job and I was granted the two weeks that I asked for. When I got home, Roy was a regular visitor; strange how fate has a way of altering one's plans. Ever since that first time I met him, I kept hoping that someday he might wake up to the fact that I was pretty nice and take a real liking to me. Strange as it may seem, he had been thinking the same about me. It didn't take him long to convince me that I would make a better farmer's wife than secretary, so I gave up the idea of going back and started in cooking for threshers.

Roy had a threshing rig of his own. There was no eight hour day then; the whistle blew at six in the morning and seven at night and afterwards he had to grease and repair. However, he came to see me every night and, shortly, we planned on getting married as soon as the work was finished. It was fun planning a new addition to the house, with a hot air furnace in the basement. We were one of the first to have central heating installed in our home.

We were married in Edmonton, Alberta, on the eleventh of December 1920 and spent most of a three week's honeymoon there and in Wetaskiwin. It was bitter cold and we were waiting for a break in the weather before going home.

Roy had a partner by the name of Henry Davis. They batched together for ten years before we were married, as their homesteads were right across the road from each other. Henry had planned to have our house in tip-top shape when we returned but instead we took him by surprise and caught him in the worst mess imaginable. The ashes had accumulated in the stove until it refused to draw; then, all of a sudden, he decided to clean them out. For some reason, the ash pan slipped out of his fingers spilling ashes all over the floor and about this time we walked in. We couldn't see a thing for dust. When it cleared away and set-tled enough for us to see the table, he had prepared some hotcakes for supper which were stiff enough to stand alone and, to top it all off, he had cut the beefsteak with the grain, making it so tough that it was impossible to eat. Martin happened to be there and he thought it all a big joke but it proved too much for Henry, so he grabbed his cap and out the door he went slamming it behind him. We didn't see a sign of him for three days.

Our wedding dance was held at the Nose Hill School. We had bought a new song in Edmonton, entitled "Let the Rest of the World Go By," which Roy and I sang during intermission. It seemed most appro-priate for the occasion and ever since we have thought of it as our song.

Henry stayed with us for another year, which enabled him to get situated comfortably on his own place. Most of the animals they had were owned jointly and had to be divided. Henry loved dogs and accu-mulated several, all of questionable ancestry. They went with him when he moved but when it came to the old mom cat, she was in a quandary where to stay. Being loyal to each of them, she settled it herself by divid-ing her time equally between them. She moved over with Henry in the spring and had her batch of kittens, then as soon as the first cold spell set in, she moved her entire family over to our place for the winter. Henry carried her back to his place many times but as soon as he turned her out she was right back to our place. She kept this up for many years until she finally died.

Roy was anxious to have us start out right and insisted on every-thing we owned belonging to both of us, instead of a this–is–mine and that–is–yours arrangement, as is often the case among married couples. I had several head of cattle, as well as my saddlehorse at home that I had to do something about. Ole, who was most generous with anything he had, gave me his monthly paycheck as a wedding present; in turn, I told him that he could have my cows. We had been used to sharing every-thing we had with each other from the time we were small and contin-ued to do the same when we grew up and thought nothing of it. The saddlehorse I reluctantly left for Papa to ride. Roy had plenty of horses, so a short while after we were married, we rode out on the range to look them over and see if we had any good prospect for a saddlehorse for me.

We hazed the bunch of horses on home and into the corral where we picked out a three-year-old filly as a possibility, cut out the rest, then roped and snubbed her to another saddlehorse and proceeded to halter-break her. She had never had a rope on her since she was branded. We could tell right away that she would be the doggy type since she responded very well without a fight. Before long we had the saddle on her and Roy climbed on. She bucked a few jumps at first, just sort of a rocking-chair buck, but after he had ridden her a few rounds, I got on her and we played with her that afternoon until she was quite gentle by evening. Before many days she was like an old cow-pony. We kept her under the saddle for many years; she would jog along, as if half asleep, until a tumbling mustard happened to come drifting along or, seeing a big rock all of a sudden, Nitchie would then shy unmercifully. Most of the time, she caught the rider unaware and if he weren't a good rider he would invariably hit the ground. She did not run away but just stopped and waited for him to climb on again.

Most of the boys we had working for us came from eastern Canada. They were grand fellows in many ways but they did not know much about branding calves and such for they were not too familiar with the range. It came in mighty handy at times when I heard Roy yell for me to come that I had knowledge of such things and could be of help to him when it was badly needed. Every rancher had his own brand; usually it was the same brand for both horses and cattle, only located on a different part of the animal and slightly changed. Our cattle brand, for instance, was quarter L lazy S, on the right rib; the horse brand was quarter circle LS on the right shoulder. The brands are registered with the government and owned exclusively by the person to whom they are assigned. It is the only way one can legally claim an animal, in case it gets lost or stolen.

One day when Roy was out riding, he came across a fellow in a 1914 model T Ford out on the Goose Lake Range. He had used the car in preference to a saddlehorse to take a look at his stock this day. Mr. McDonald wasn't much of a mechanic. In fact, he didn't know the first thing about a car, so when it stopped on him for no particular reason, as he thought, and miles from anywhere, he was very upset and proceeded to get very angry and offered to trade it for Roy's saddlehorse. The deal was made and Roy hauled it home. He went to work on it and before long had it hitting on all four. It was far from perfect but it was a car. It took a real strong man to crank it to get it started. People used to ask us why we kept it on top of the hill behind the house but we had good reason for that, for when we were ready to go somewhere, all we had to do was to give it a push and jump in. The brakes were none too good either; we had to make sure the gate was wide open to give us clear sailing on out to the road where we would keep on travelling until we got to our destination, then stop on a hill again. It was the forerunner of the sports model; no top and just one seat with a box behind. After a complete overhaul with new repairs, including a high-speed gear, it had plenty of pep and we could really go places. I learned to drive old Lizzie before long but I lacked complete faith in it and would go back to my trusty saddlehorse for safe conveyance when I wanted to be sure to get someplace.

If it happened to rain and we had forgotten to bring the coils into the house, we were out of luck for a while. We then had to put them in the oven and wait until they dried out before we could start the motor. Nevertheless, we had a lot of fun with it and kept Lizzie for many years as a relic.

Chapter XIV

The first well that we dug on the place was abandoned when we hit quicksand at twenty-two feet and a foot of water had seeped in. It was curbed with lumber but considered a total loss until we hit upon the idea of making it into an ice-well, and it made a grand one. It measured four by four feet square, with a ladder nailed on to one side that extended all the way to the bottom. This was the only refrigerator we had and the ladder enabled us to climb down to the ice which kept getting lower as it melted. We kept all perishables in a box that had a rope attached to it and a windlass to wind it up or let it down. Every winter the men sawed big blocks of ice on one of the sloughs, then hauled and dumped them into the well until it was filled to the top. We built a little house over it and were never without ice, for it lasted from one year to the next. We had plenty of cream and the men were always willing to turn the ice cream freezer or help with the eating part as well. Whenever I hear the word deep-freeze mentioned, it reminds me of the old ice-well and the many ice cream parties we used to enjoy.

Alkali was quite common in our part of the country. One could easily spot an alkali slough by the white ring around it and the water had a peculiar, bad taste. In a dry year, as the water in the slough receded, the white ring got bigger. When the water dried up completely, it formed a white dust that drifted with the wind and was hard on a person's skin. It made our lips crack and eyes smart, if you happened to be in the path of it. Cattle and horses would pass up these watering places for a fresh spring and we were equally careful when filling our deep-freeze, not to get any ice blocks from an alkali slough.

The first picnic we had in Nose Hills was held on Zeedyk's place, a little north and below where the school now stands. This one was the forerunner of the annual picnic that took place on the third of June after that. There was no road except the old wagon trail that wound around the hills, so the picnic had to be held where the people could get to it without climbing a mountain. The men worked real hard to prepare for the event. They had to build a corral for the bucking contest which was the main feature; then there was racing and baseball. The old trail was quite straight for some distance here and served nicely as a race track for the horse races. The three teams competing in the baseball tournament were Nose Hill, Loyalist and Bar-O-Five.

Each of us rode horseback to the picnic, for Roy had charge of the racing program and needed his saddlehorse during the day. Several races were scheduled and run. When it came time for the ladies' horse race, Roy rode up to the booth where I was working and asked me to come on and get in the race. There were only two other entries, the Lewis sisters from Battle Bend, whose horses belonged to the same family. They were real running horses; mine was just a good saddlehorse. The men, as usual, were having fun placing bets on the winner. Roy warned me to watch out for the first jump, for he had started every race with Mick, spurring him for a fast getaway. Competition is a great game even among animals. As soon as we got lined up and Roy hollered "go," Mick jumped about ten feet and was off, for he no doubt was expecting a sharp prod of the spur. This gave us a good lead and we managed to nose out the other horses and win the race. The local boys were surprised as well as happy with their winnings and I of course was happy to have won.

We were real lucky that day. Besides the horse race I won the ladies' foot race and was awarded a fine box-camera which was the first one I ever owned. Roy won the high jump and the long throw with a baseball. There were many competitions; Ray Coates took the championship in the bucking contest. Among the other contestants were Bob Ford, Bannard Vetter and George Stevens. Good sportsmanship prevailed throughout the day. After this was over we rode on home to do the chores, then dressed and drove back to the school house to join the rest of the crowd and finish the day by dancing until the wee hours in the morning.

The wagon trail mentioned was part of the old Klondike Trail used by the Red River Carts on their way from Winnipeg to Edmonton in the early days. It was different from the ordinary road in that it had three ruts. Besides the wagon tracks, there was a path in the center made by a single ox or horse hitched to the cart. Most of it has disappeared under the plow but a trace of it can still be found in our front yard.

We were very happy and luck seemed to be with us. The first year passed quickly, then just after Christmas our baby was born; a fine big boy whom we named Lyal. His arrival happened during a bitterly cold spell that kept Roy busy firing the furnace and kitchen stove, doing the chores and looking after us. When he finally made it to town he found that our credit was, indeed, good with Bill Price at the Veteran Hotel. The boys did not wait for Roy but they took it upon themselves to celebrate without him and had consumed the equivalent of twenty-five dollars worth of various brands during their felicitations and best wishes for health and happiness for the new son and heir. He was a fine baby and we took him with us wherever we went. At six weeks, he attended his first dance in his basket and went regularly after that. At six months of age, he went with us to the Battle River Stampede and camped out for several days. We had no formula to bother with and no bottles to sterilize which eliminated a lot of work and worry and he really thrived on mother's milk.

Every Thursday was hog shipping day in Veteran. A lot of queer things could and did happen on such days. Roy and Zebb Witt took a load of our hogs to town on Thursday morning. When they had not returned home by ten o'clock that night, I called it a day and went to bed. About one o'clock I heard a racket out in the kitchen and quickly lit the lamp to find out what was going on. There were Roy and Zebb rolling a very nice baby buggy back and forth. It seemed that there had been a sale of household goods in town that day and as a joke the baby buggy was knocked down to a bachelor who lived in a house known as the Orphan's Home with three other young men. The fellows must have had a big time wheeling the baby buggy up and down the street, explaining details in connection with it as well as recommending the young man who was supposed to have bought it to every young girl they saw. Finally someone got the bright idea that we needed one and put it in Roy's wagon. It did not belong to anyone in particular and since we really did need one they brought it on home. At least that was their version of it. Zebb was afraid to go home that night, so I made a bed for him on the couch in the living room and after finishing off a big pot of strong black coffee, we all retired once more.

The next morning George Rolls called up and asked if I happened to know the whereabouts of a baby buggy. He was the young man who was supposed to have bought it. I assured him that I did; the incident was a huge joke but a practical one. George never forgot the affair; when he later married and his own children came along, he must have decided it had served its purpose and bought himself a new one. When our babies grew up and we had no more use for a buggy, I let another family have it; it was handed down three times that I know of. It turned out to be one of the most sensible things that ever happened on Hog Day in Veteran.

The years rolled by and in a little less than two years our second baby arrived. This time it was a lovely little girl, just what we had hoped for. We named her Eleanor Marie, after both of her grandmothers. My Mother's name was the eighth Marie in successive generations in my Mother's family.

Chapter XV

Roy's folks kept writing and urging us to come to Maryland for a visit. I was reluctant to travel that far with two little children, the youngest only fourteen months. However Christmas Day found us enjoying the sunny south with his family. It was my first green Christmas and I couldn't quite get used to having no snow and cold weather at this time of year.

Marie made a big hit with everybody, especially her grandmother. Besides being pretty, she was real smart for her age, partly because of the training that Louie Brett, our school teacher, gave her. Louie stayed with us and she spent hours trying to teach Marie to talk, even before she could walk, and succeeded in doing it. When grandmother sewed, Marie insisted on "shoing shom, too." She worked on a wad of material with a darning needle and thread, pulling it in and out, until it knotted into a bunch. This little knot grandmother kept in her sewing basket as long as she lived.

I was real tired when we got back home in the spring and I promised myself that I would never leave the place again. Another year passed quickly and Lyal was now five; he was a big boy for his age and our pride and joy. I was watching the children at play from the pantry window one morning when suddenly Lyal fell and couldn't seem to get back on his feet. I hurried out to see what was the trouble and found that he had lost the use of his legs that quick. I carried him into the house and felt that he had some fever, so I phoned for Dr. Lander. He came right away and pronounced it some kind of paralysis. If it were infantile paralysis he would have to be put in a cast, the Doctor said. I had heard my Mother say many times that heat or cold would do wonders, along with massage. It was if she were speaking to me from the grave.

I went to work right away with hot, wet applications and kept him wrapped in wool and massaged his legs almost continuously. At the end of six weeks we could notice some signs of improvement and that gave us hope that he might be able to walk again. We were at our wits end when Roy suggested that we go to California for the winter and see what the sunshine and warm weather would do for him. As soon as threshing and grain-hauling were finished, we packed our bags, locked up the house and headed south. The change worked wonders; I kept up my routine massage and this, together with the warm sunshine and orange juice he consumed, must have helped for his muscles began to strengthen and before long he could walk some.

It turned out to be a fine vacation after all. We bought an old seven-passenger Buick and toured most of southern California in it. Then in the spring, we drove to the Canadian line where we sold the car for more than we had originally paid for it. The most wonderful result of the whole trip was that Lyal was responding to treatment. The first thing we did when we got home was to buy him a tricycle. Roy kept raising the seat to where Lyal could barely touch the pedals; in that way we hoped to straighten the knees as well as strengthen the leg muscles. Marie would stand on the bar at the back of the tricycle and hold on to him and they rode around the dining room table until they wore a path in our new rug.

I was rewarded a hundred-fold for the many hours of twisting hot, wet towels and massaging until my hands were red and sore, when Roy and I attended his graduation in 1944 at the University of Maryland. Afterwards he passed the U.S. Navy's medical examination without a question. It has always been a mystery to us how he picked up the germ in such an isolated place.

Doctor Little was one of the finest humanitarians. Besides being everybody's family doctor, he was the best friend one could wish for. He had the welfare of his patients at heart and no road was too long nor a storm too severe for him to face when a person was in need of his help. I heard him say that in all the years he had practised in Veteran, he had never lost a mother.

Dr. Lander, who succeeded him, was also a real pioneer. Neither one had any of the facilities to work with that the medical profession of today enjoys. They had real human interest and the welfare of man at heart and this in my estimation is the most important quality in a man on whom you need to depend to save your life at times.

I remember one time in particular. It was nearly midnight when our phone rang and Elmo Dowker, our neighbor, asked if I could come over to Larsen's right away, as Yoland was very sick and he was afraid she would die before morning. It was a bitterly cold night, at least forty below zero outside. I wanted to ride horseback but Roy wouldn't hear of it. He hitched the team to the cutter while I dressed and collected the necessary supplies to take with me; these were thermometer, hot water bottle with attachments, ice bag, a white apron and a loaf of fresh bread. When we got there Dr. Lander was walking the floor, still dressed in his buffalo overcoat, mittens and muskrat cap. It was beastly cold in the house and the five little children were huddled around the stove with the husband, who was just getting over a spell of sickness, trying to keep the fire going. After examining her, the Doctor decided that he must operate and that called for another Doctor to assist. It was twenty-five miles to Coronation but after telephoning the Doctor there he promised to meet Roy at Talbot, which was half way. The horses had to plunge through snowdrifts to break the road all the way, which made it difficult to make time.

After waiting a couple of hours, Dr. Lander decided that his patient could not wait any longer, so stripped down to his shirt sleeves in that cold house and went to work. I had already sterilized the instruments in an old dishpan that jiggled and jumped all over the stove and made such a racket that she could not stand it and begged us to let her alone and let her die. I held on to the pan the best I could to keep it still until the instruments were considered sterile, then placed them on my clean white apron that I spread over a chair next to the bed and we started. I held the coal oil lamp, which was the only light there was, first in one hand, then in the other, until I thought my arms would drop off; it took over an hour before we finished. Then, about five o'clock in the morning, Roy drove in with the other Doctor and both were nearly frozen. They were glad it was all over. Both Doctors agreed that it was a mercy operation and that she had only a thousand-to-one chance to survive. Evidently all she needed was that one chance for she pulled through. Next morning Dr. Lander drove back to our place and went to bed for a while so as to get some rest before starting back to town where no doubt there was another call waiting for him. I stayed on as nurse for two more days without sleep, then Mrs. Dunn, another neighbor, took over and let me go home for a much-needed rest. Besides sickness, the Larsen family had experienced the misfortune of having their home destroyed by fire, including all the contents; still they were too proud to ask for assistance.

Chapter XVI

Sam Harper was one of our neighbors who could be described as a character. He was quite old when he came into the district and homesteaded one of the roughest quarter sections in the hills. His land adjoined the school yard and, seeing the need for a pasture for the many horses that the children rode to school, he donated part of his land for this purpose. At one time there were fifteen saddlehorses along with sixteen children attending our school. He sold his land soon after he had proved up and left for the States to spend the rest of his days. In about two months he was back; he moved into a vacant shack up on the corner south of us and this is still referred to as Sam's Corner.

He came over to see us real often and we supplied him with eggs and bacon for many years without a thought of remuneration, either by him or us. He was a real card shark, for his age, at whist, bridge or penny ante, the last being his favorite game. We had to use real strategy to compete with him. He would never quit until he was ahead, so if his luck was against him, we simply had to let him win to get rid of him when it was time for him to go home. He loved to play jokes on the rest of us too. One cold winter night he crept up to the pantry window outside the house while I was preparing supper and jumped up in front of me and gave a yell. His coal-black beady eyes and snow-white beard encased in a muskrat cap along with that yell startled me so that I dropped my salad bowl and broke it. Sam was in the dog house for a while; the next day he brought over a freshly baked gooseberry pie to make up for it.

He always insisted on me as his card partner when playing whist or bridge and I got tired of it. One night there was to be a whist drive or party at the schoolhouse. There were at least forty people who drew for partners for the evening, so I thought to myself that this is one time when I won't have to play with old Sam. When all had drawn numbers and were comparing them to find their partners, here came old Sam. Sure enough, I was it. He chuckled and with a twinkle in his eye said, "You thought that this time you would get rid of me, didn't you? Never mind; we will cop the prize, you'll see," and we did.

There was plenty to do on the farm in those days. We did not have the facilities or conveniences of today. Most of us had several hired men to cook for besides the regular family. It was the custom to wash and iron their clothes and often they expected to get their patching done as well, which we did.

Along about this time, Britain found it difficult to care for all her unemployed, so for several years hundreds of young men arrived in Canada looking for a place to stay over the winter. The Canadian farmers were asked to give these young men a home and train them in the rudiments of farming or ranching, which would make them useful citizens on the prairie. We did not need any extra help in winter but most farmers took one and sometimes two. In addition to their regular keep, they were to receive five dollars a month for spending money plus free smoking tobacco. Nearly all were city boys and not much help to the average farmer the first year. They were well-mannered fellows and most helpful about the house which was an inducement for the housewife to agree to the extra boarder. One such young man we had and incidentally grew very fond of was Scottie. He was supposed to bring a team of horses to the field one morning. After struggling with the harness for about an hour he came to the house and asked me to help him. He claimed that the harness would not fit the horses for some reason and when I got to the barn, I could readily see why. The collar was on backward and the hames upside down.

These boys, not being used to the best, were easily pleased. They had tremendous appetites and praised the food as well as the wonderful cooks of western Canada. We cooked good wholesome meals with what we grew on the farm and baked big batches of bread and rolls twice a week, besides pies and cakes every day. We churned our own butter and canned enough fruit to last a whole year; much of our fruit was wild berries that we picked ourselves. We always grew a big garden and enough potatoes to supply several families. In the fall, when all harvesting was done, it was a joy to go down in the cellar and look at the results of our efforts: bins of all the different kinds of vegetables buried in sand, rows of canned fruit, jars of pickles and preserves and a dozen or more boxes of apples. Among the kinds were luscious Mackintosh Reds, Grimes Golden, Snow and Rabbit Nose, all giving off the scent of the orchard and competing with the thirty gallon crock of sauerkraut in the corner.

Hens refused to lay in winter so to substitute for the fresh eggs that we didn't have, we preserved a ten gallon crock full in a solution called waterglass. Every fall it took a lot of energy to prepare for winter but once it was done we had a bountiful supply and one or two extra around the table didn't seem to matter.

Roy's cousin, George Merriken, from California paid us an unexpected visit one summer. He was a college student, raised on the city pavement and green to the ways of the west. In Alberta, where there was such a scarcity of women, our men realized how hard we had to work and were most helpful in every way. George was a demanding fellow. The first day he happened to smell some onions cooking. He immediately notified me that he did not tolerate that particular specimen of the vegetable family and not to put any in his food. I in turn was not used to being dictated to, so I pointed out to him right then that our cook car was not in use and was fully equipped. If he didn't like my cooking, he was welcome to use it and cook to suit himself.

The next day he decided to go for a horseback ride. He climbed on Nitchie on the wrong side, which happens to be the right side of the horse. She didn't like the idea and walked slowly over to the slough in the barnyard and gave a heave. George landed in the mud, head first. His white corduroy pants changed to muddy grey and they were never the same again. George was a smart lad and caught on fast. He had a three months visitor's permit and when his time was up begged us to help him get an extension. By this time we had grown real fond of him, so we all piled into our new Pontiac and headed for Calgary. Incidentally, it was Stampede week and that in itself was a big thrill. We stayed until the finish and during this time got his extension, which made him real happy and enabled him to spend another thirty days with us.

Several years later we went to California again. George was now married and lived on a lovely citrus ranch. We went to see him and while there he invited me to go with him to pick a bucketful of oranges. On our way to the orchard he stopped for a moment and said, "Shorty, I want to thank you for what you did for me up in Alberta." I couldn't imagine what he was referring to, so I asked him and his answer was, "Oh, everything. To sum it up in a nutshell, you taught me to eat onions."

Chapter XVII

Every summer we planned on taking in the Old Timers' Picnic at Clark's Lake twenty miles north of us for our vacation. To be eligible for membership in this organization it was necessary to have been a resident of the community for at least twenty years. This picnic usually lasted four days with no special program for entertainment although there seemed to be something going on most of the time, such as horseshoe-pitching, basketball and an occasional game of baseball and swimming. People came here mostly for relaxation and to visit.

Fred Davis, one of our old bachelor neighbors, always accompanied us and would bring along a huge smoked ham as his contribution to the lunch basket. Before leaving home, I cooked and baked up enough food to last us for the duration. The best part of this outing for me was that Roy and Fred did most of the work. We had breakfast of bacon and eggs cooked over a camp fire, along with a big pot of coffee and toast on spits. They seemed to enjoy doing this, even to washing the dishes afterwards. In the evening, everyone there enjoyed buffalo barbecue, for which the Government donated the buffalo meat. Potatoes were boiled in fifty gallon drums and served with the meat along with all the coffee we wanted, free of charge. There was the dance platform in the open for those who enjoyed dancing, with a fine old-time string orchestra; the young people really took over after the sun went down.

We were sitting around the campfire one evening when some youngsters drove up to tell us that a hailstorm had hit our community late that afternoon and had wrecked the crops in the whole district. It made us sick at heart; we gathered our belongings, took the children and hurried home as fast as we could. Neither of us spoke a word all the way. About five miles from home we began to run into the destruction the hail had done. We saw crops flattened and fields ruined all along the road. When we reached the corner of our land we could hardly believe our eyes. There stood our lovely wheat crop untouched, swaying in the breeze. Roy stopped the car and we both got out and walked hand in hand into the field. I was trying hard to keep the tears back, when finally Roy said, "Let's go back and finish our vacation," which we did. The hailstorm came within a few hundred yards of our place.

Another annual outing was berry picking. We depended on our neighbors, the Dowkers, to know where to find the best saskatoons and to organize a party for a day in the hills. About eight or ten of us used to pile into a wagon loaded with cream cans and tubs to hold the berries and huge baskets of lunch, plus gallon jugs of coffee and off we went to the hills. The horses had to pull hard to get us up and down those steep sidehills and into coulees where the choicest berries were found. This was also a picnic and we took plenty of time for eating our lunch leisurely at noon and again before we left for home. With every container filled with berries we landed home about sundown, tired but happy in the thought of an enjoyable day well spent.

The real work started the next morning when I had to clean and can the berries. We tried to get a hundred quarts put up, mostly for the cook car at harvesting and threshing time. I did not always make my quota; nevertheless none went to waste. We had a large stone crock and, when I got to the limit of my endurance, I dumped the rest into the crock for wine. Saskatoons make the best wine imaginable. We always intended to save the wine for Christmas but it had a way of disappearing somehow and by the time the holidays rolled around, the keg was usually empty.

There was something magic about the hills. In winter it was always several degrees warmer where we lived than on the flats below. We seemed to get better crops, too, and were not subject to early frost, being much higher; nor hail, like the country around us. There was good shelter for cattle in winter and shade in summer and a haven for jack rabbits. Some winters they were so numerous that we had to fence our haystacks with poultry wire to keep the rabbits from eating up the hay. Clumps of silver willow, buck brush and roseberry patches provided both cover and food for the many Hungarian quail and prairie chickens.

I have been told that Nose Hills was the camping ground and home of a tribe of Indians for many years before the white man took over. We found numerous signs of encampments as we roamed about. There was a legend which claimed that buffalo were pushed over a steep cliff, which we called Buffalo Fall, by riders. In their fright the huge animals lost their footing and some would tumble to the bottom, a drop of nearly two hundred feet, piling on top of each other. Some would be crippled and fall prey to the hunter. There was a big pile of bones at the bottom which somewhat substantiated the legend. However, the white man must take most of the blame for the disappearance of the buffalo.

The eagle's nest was another attraction. A pair of bald eagles made their nest in the hills for many years. We did not molest these birds.

They had a wing spread of over six feet and claws so strong that they could pick up a lamb and carry it to their nest without any apparent effort. The young eaglets left our part of the country as soon as they could shift for themselves but the old pair came back every year to nest in the same place.

My fondness for the hills is best described in the following poem, which I wrote many years ago.

THE FRIENDLY HILLS

The Hills, how comforting to see
When on a journey and I'm nearing home.
This clear and rugged outline 'gainst the sky
And on their snow white crest and snowcaps high
I gaze in ecstasy, 'tis home to me!

Like stalwart sentinels they stand and guard
A little house tucked in among the trees.
And tho' the journey's been both long and hard,
My heart beats quicker when that light I see,
And through the stormy night it beckons me.

In summer, it's the same. I love to stroll
Along paths, and dream of other days gone by;
To watch the beauty from a distant knoll
Of woodland covered hills that greet the eye
And bring contentment to a weary soul.

To hear the blackbirds chirp, the robin's song;
The old hawk's piercing shriek from out the sky;
The branches bent with berries; perfume strong
From flowers wild; a rabbit hurrying by,
And softly crooning breezes whispering nigh.

I love to linger when the setting sun
Sends up its rays of gold and crimson hue.
I find contentment when day's work is done;
To watch the mellow twilight stealing through
And bring forth cherished memories anew.
This is the place I like to live; and when
I journey forth from here to distant shore
I have a wish—think not that I pretend –
I ask no more, grant me this one request,
Beneath these friendly hills, lay me to rest.

Chapter XVIII

The cattlemen and horse ranchers held sway until the home-steaders closed in on them and began to put up fences. This is the period that I like to remember; nothing but rolling prairie dotted here and there with herds of cattle and horses. Sometimes an occasional rider could be seen sauntering toward some bunch to read the brand and find out what ranch they belonged to. Quite often a rancher owned only the quarter section where his buildings and corrals were and utilized the rest of the territory around him for grazing and feed for his stock, at no expense. Until the land was settled there were no taxes and no bound-aries to the grazing privileges; this however did not help the government and they were anxious to get settlers on the land. When we first home-steaded, the tax on our one hundred and sixty acres was two dollars per year; later on it was raised to five. This kind of revenue did not enable the government to do much, consequently it was many years before we got any improvements such as roads.

As long as we could follow a trail across the prairie, we got along fine but, when fences began to appear and cut off the trails, we had to follow the road allowance according to geographical surveys; then roads became a necessity. It is interesting to compare the methods used, then and now, in road construction. In the early days, a road crew consisted of the boss, three four-horse teams on fresnos and one plow team that was also responsible for floating the road or grade to smooth it off before it could pass inspection. A man with a four-horse team earned seventy-five cents an hour, or seven dollars and fifty cents for a ten hour day, which was applied on back taxes. When one man had earned enough to clear up his tax bill, another taxpayer took his place and so it went on until the small allotment for this section was used up. Each district was desig-nated a certain territory to work.

Roy was road boss in our district for a number of years. After completing the assignment, there was a certain amount of grading to be done. It took twelve horses to pull the big grader and my brother, Martin, was the teamster. It took real skill and know-how to handle three four-horse teams strung out and to be able to turn that outfit around time and again on a grade, to say nothing about manipulating a grader under such circumstances. It was surprising the amount of road work that was accom-plished with almost no money and the limited amount of machinery to work with. This was the beginning of better roads in our community.

Roy was very resourceful and a hard worker. He could do most anything and do it well. He could play just as hard if the opportunity presented itself, especially if it had anything to do with baseball. He was a good pitcher and the different teams used to come after him when there was a tournament or on picnic days. The children and I went along, too; they used to love it.

One fall, when Lyal and Marie were four and two respectively, our cook on the cook car quit. It was bitterly cold weather; we had a threshing rig of our own and tried to get as much outside work done as possible, leaving our own crop to the last. Cooks were scarce and I had to come to the rescue and finish up the season. We had a section of land rented, which is six hundred and forty acres, three miles from home. There was a good crop of wheat. In fact, it was a bumper crop and we had to get it threshed. I bundled up the kids and took them with me every morning and we got home about nine o'clock at night. I had ten men to cook for; they had to have four meals a day and hot coffee on the stove at all times. The cook car was close to the separator, which made it handy for the boys to run in and get a piece of pie or lunch any-time and always a cup of coffee.

It is a race with nature towards the end of the season when the restless clouds start milling around and close in on you like a thick blanket. The wind howls and carries a nasty sting and the icy blast penetrates to the bone. The boys built little bonfires to keep warm while waiting for their turn to pitch off their loads. We had been threshing for six days and had one day's work left and that happened to be Sunday. Roy asked the crew what they wanted to do; they were all anxious to get home so voted to work and finish the job. Toward evening I went home to pre-pare supper. We had promised them a big turkey dinner as a climax; besides, I was glad to get home again with the children.

It was eleven o'clock that night before I heard the chug of the engine in the distance. What a grand feeling to see it pull into the yard with the separator; then the cook car, bunk car, junk wagon and eight bundle teams with racks followed. Soon there was lots of excitement around the yard, getting the horses unhitched and fed, and by the time the last man had washed and was ready to sit down to the table, it was midnight. I had ample time to get a big turkey dinner with all the trim-mings that I could think of. The crew had worked eighteen hours that day but a livelier bunch of fellows I have never seen. A few of the men went on to their homes towards morning; the rest went out to the bunk car and rolled in. When we woke up the next day the ground was covered with six inches of snow. We were snowed in for the winter from then on.

The first of November was called due-date. This was the date when all accounts had to be paid. Notes became due; bank loans, machinery debts, taxes and grocery bills all became due at the same time. As soon as the grain wagon started rolling, merchants began to look for their money. A lot of credit was extended during the summer and fall, especially if the crop looked promising. It was not unusual for anyone with a cook car to have a six hundred dollar grocery bill at the end of the season. Not many farmers were able to hold their wheat until spring when the price was better.

Roy started hauling wheat as soon as threshing was finished. He drove a six-horse team to two wagons, a grain tank ahead with a triple box behind, hauling two hundred bushels at a time and making a trip to town every day. It was twelve miles and a half; it took a pretty tough outfit of horses to cover twenty-five miles every day. He made twenty-six trips one month. It was during this period, while I was waiting for him to get home one evening, that I wrote the following poem, dedicated to Roy and other grain haulers who had to hit the frozen trail.

ON THE TRAIL

How still the evening, and crisp the crunching snow;
The air is oh, so cold! and dusk is near,
Gone are the rays of the sunset's golden glow
And one by one the lonely stars appear.

Dim lights shine forth from homes across the plain
Like scattered jewels on a glittering coat.
A coyote's mournful wail, now and again;
White smoke from poplars, green, through chimneys float.

We're homeward bound, the faithful six and I,
Trail weary from the daily trips we make
With golden grain on which we must rely
For food and shelter, health, and comfort's sake.

The Hills are now in sight, with snow capped peaks
Like wise old sages, silvered with the years,
Undaunted, too, through centuries they seek
To guide the lost, and still the wanderer's fears.

We're round the bend. Ah! there's the light, it seems
To shine a little brighter than the rest.
The Northern lights in gorgeous colors gleam,
And sounds of sleigh bells drift from yonder crest.

I've visions of a fireside bright with cheer,
A fond caress, warmth, food, and love untold,
Companionship, so sweet, from one so dear!
Ah! these to me are worth far more than gold.

We're home. The six stand patiently demure.
I'm numb. Their frosty coats tell their own tale.
Forgotten, soon, are hardships we endure
And solitude along the long, long trail.

Chapter XIX

Most of our wheat went to the United Grain Growers elevator. This, I believe, was the first cooperative marketing venture the farmers of Alberta undertook and it proved very successful. My Dad bought some of the first issues of shares from Rice Jones, who drove all over the country trying to interest farmers in cooperation. Later Mr. Jones held a high executive position with the U.G.G. Elevator Company.

Cooperatives are nearly always created because of necessity. We were again grasping at straws when the Alberta Wheat Pool was organized. This farmer-owned grain-buying cooperative has been a blessing to agriculture in Alberta. It has one of the largest and most modern grain terminals in the world at Vancouver, B.C. The Pool is a good example of what can be accomplished if enough people stick together and all work toward a common goal.

After I got married, the menfolk at home were left to batch, but not for very long. Papa went to Bellingham for a visit and while there got married. Ole followed suit by marrying Gina Bakken. Then, a short while later, Martin and Julia Bakken were married. If there had been any more boys in our family, I am sure they all would have married Bakken girls; there were still two younger ones left. All four were beautiful girls.

When the Lutheran church had its hundredth year of celebration at Camrose in 1925, Ole, Gina and their children, Kenney and Norma, along with us and our two, took in a whole week of festivities. We all went in one car and brought our tent along so as to have a place to camp. We also did some campfire cooking on the side, to the delight of some of our relatives whom we met at the Conference. The children enjoyed the outing as much as we did. They were all under four years of age and no trouble whatever to take along.

The most tragic thing in our young life happened in 1927 when Ole caught a bad cold; pneumonia set in and he suddenly died. I felt as if a part of me had gone with him. I missed him terribly and anything we tried to do afterward was not the same. I am sure the rest of our family felt the same way. Gina was left with three little children; Marvin, the youngest one, was only seven months old at the time.

When Lyal first started to school he rode on the back of Harold Witt's bike. Before long he wanted to ride horseback like most of the other children. We had one old workhorse that we thought might be trusty enough, for they are more dependable than an old saddlehorse and not so cagey. Rastus was safe, though also stubborn. They started out fine but in about an hour's time they came back with Lyal crying and pulling on the reins. Rastus was taking it in his stride, which was not very fast, but determined. They had gotten as far as the schoolhouse gate when Rastus decided to turn around and go home. There was nothing a six-year-old could do but sit there and take it.

We then bought an old mare, Dolly, that had been taking kids to school for fifteen years. She knew exactly where to go. When she got to the school, she turned in, be that Sunday or Monday. We had plenty of horses but none gentle enough for little children. When Lyal and Marie got a little older and learned to ride, they each had a lovely pony of their own which they rode to school.

Our third baby came along when the other two were old enough to attend school. She was a lovely little girl with golden hair. We named her Jean. She did not resemble the other two very much; they had dark hair and looked more like Roy. We called Jean the golden girl. When she got older and could talk, she was forever reminding me that, "Sis is not the golden girl; I'm the golden girl," and I always agreed with her. When she kept on asking me repeatedly such questions as "Are you glad you got me?" and had me point out to her where she was born and if her nose was like her grandfather's and so on, I finally became curious. It boiled down to the fact that since she was so much younger than Lyal and Marie and didn't resemble them in looks, she feared that she might have been adopted and was finding out for herself. I had to convince her that she was quite authentic and one of the family.

Marie was a studious child and particularly interested in literature. She would sometimes leave her playmates and go to her room to finish a story which she was reading; she was equally fond of poetry. On one occasion, when a group of children were playing hide and seek, she could not be found. I went to look for her and found her in her room reading poetry. When I came in she looked up at me with a dreamy, far-away look in her eyes and said, "Safe upon the solid rock the ugly houses stand. That's you, mother." I knew what she meant but, just to make a joke of it, I said "So, you think I'm ugly, do you?" I was sorry for that remark and had to do a lot of cuddling before we got things back to normal. She was only eight years old when this happened.

All school teachers have my admiration and sympathy. Especially the ones who braved all kinds of weather to get to the little country school on the prairie on bitter, frosty mornings. Some even acted as their own janitor, building the fire to get the place warm before the children arrived. In winter it was often difficult to keep warm. There were times when the children had to huddle around the stove with their lessons until the room temperature moderated. Nevertheless, the knowledge gained was not impaired in any way. I fully believe there is a decided advantage in a small school where the children get individual instruction. At least I found it so. The teacher in a one room country school taught eight grades, most often it was nine, and occasionally helped a student with the tenth grade. She was not compelled to teach beyond the eighth grade but most of them were willing to help a student who did not have the opportunity to go on with their education, even though it meant extra work and longer hours. The teachers were competing for honors, too, through their pupils. This was most evident at the Annual School Fair each fall when fourteen schools competed in all activities from public speaking, art, singing, literature and composition, to all kinds of agriculture projects.

The month of December was devoted to practising for the Christmas concert. It served as the climax of the year's training in drama, speech and singing. On this particular night the school house would be packed to capacity to watch the little performers do their very best, to the enjoyment of all and the pride of the parents. The real meaning of Christmas, the birth of the Christ Child, had a prominent place on the program and every child had a part of some kind. Santa always managed to get there at the right time. The children listened intently for the sound of sleigh bells which they knew would announce his coming; the little ones could hardly wait. It was fascinating to see them watching wide-eyed as he bounced in the door, shaking the snow off the huge packsack full of toys as he tossed it in on the floor and began pulling out all kinds of gifts, first making sure that each little recipient had been the model of good behaviour before relinquishing the brightly-wrapped package.

After a sumptuous midnight lunch the floor was cleared for dancing that lasted until daybreak or until it was light enough for the horses to follow the snow trail and take us safely home.

Chapter XX

Every fall we had a spell of lovely Indian Summer weather. I always like to think that it is Mother Nature's way of taking a vacation to rest up before going into the hazardous winter months. Ordinarily there is a good breeze blowing on the prairie, yet sometimes we have a lull of two or three days of the calmest weather imaginable with not a leaf stirring. We depend on our windmill to pump water for the stock; consequently when there was no wind there was not water in the tank. It is impossible to control animals when they are thirsty; they will break down barriers and go through fences to satisfy their thirst. The cattle and horses were no problem, for I could get on a saddlehorse and push them to a slough or spring somewhere. With pigs it is different. We had over one hundred head of Duroc Jersey pigs about ready for market. They ran in a pasture of about ten acres and we had water piped from the tank at the well to the troughs in the pig pasture. As long as the windmill was turning it kept the pigs' troughs full and running over.

Roy's Dad from Maryland was visiting us at the time when such a spell of weather occurred. The pigs began to squeal for fair the second day of the calm and he was worried, as well as impatient and tired of the continual noise. He happened to be the only man on the place, as Roy and all the rest were out on the threshing outfit. All our workhorses were also on the outfit, except a few of the older ones that we had turned out at the other place about eight miles from home. There were two saddlehorses in the barn and one old horse, balky as well as foundered, walking around the place; this one was too stiff in the front legs to run and keep up with the rest when we turned them out. The saddlehorses had never had a harness on, for one can easily spoil the gait of a good saddle horse by putting him in harness and making him pull. Any good rider would put up a fight to the finish with a man who tried to put his favorite saddlehorse into harness.

We had a five hundred gallon tank on a wagon for emergency watering and Grampy, who was about seventy years old and considered himself quite a horseman, could stand it no longer. He was going to hitch old Balky and Nitchie to the water tank and get some water on the job. I had a big notion to let him try it. He would have had a real exciting time, since neither horse would pull the hat off your head. I was afraid of the outcome and did not want him to get hurt. He was used to eastern horses and the eastern way of handling them. I feel sure that any good teamster or puncher will agree with me that the same tactics will not work with our western broncs. Even our regular workhorses would crowd into the corner of their stall and snort to beat everything when Grampy appeared in the barn door and happened to utter a couple of unfamiliar "who, whos" that they were not used to hearing.

I tried my best to convince Grampy that the wind would soon start blowing and everything would be all right—without success. His faith in the weather was not strong enough. He however compromised to the extent that he promised to leave the horses alone while I took Punch and rode the eight miles and brought back a team that I knew would pull. We hitched them to the tank wagon and drove to Unbuwusts' flowing well. There the whole family helped me fill the big tank; we formed a bucket brigade from the well to the tank in a sort of person-to-person manner. It took hundreds of pails of water to fill the tank. When I got home and backed the wagon up to the water tank at the well, opened the valve and let the water run, I thought I felt a faint breeze. Sure enough, before long, the windmill was turning; the troughs in the pig pasture were filling up fast and once more peace reigned and everything was quiet around the place, including Grampy.

Punch was our favorite saddle horse. He was a fine specimen, a mixture of Percheron and standard-bred and combined the best quality of both breeds. He really took me for a ride one day. As any real horseman knows, one cannot trust a horse completely, no matter how faithful he seems. Punch was no exception. We used a certain curved bit on him but this time the boys had taken the other ponies and bridles with them. I had to get the cows from the back field about a mile away and Punch had never been ridden without that bridle. I hated to walk that far, so I saddled him and started out with only a halter shank in my hand. I opened the gate and climbed on Punch and he took off looking for country; I hadn't the least bit of control over him.

Around the quarter-section we went in nothing flat. Nels Ranneseth's threshing outfit came down the road as we streaked by inside our fence. The men whooped and hollered at us and I'm sure they thought that I was out exercising the horse. This did not tend to quiet him any; he finally turned toward home and of all things to happen, one of the stirrups came off the saddle. There I was with one lone stirrup and the horn. That was one time that I really pulled leather.

I had to watch out for my leg to keep it from being crushed against the post as he turned in the gate into the yard and made a bee line for the water tank. About fifty feet from it, he started to skid and I really braced myself. I had kicked my other foot out of the remaining stirrup long before, so as not to get tangled up in the saddle if he should take a notion to buck. With both feet forward and both hands clasped on the horn, I was lifted out of the saddle and back several times but managed to stay with him. I attribute my luck to all the bareback riding I did as a kid. Punch just shook his head, as if that was over and nothing to it. I felt like giving him the licking of his life, but I didn't.

It came in real handy at times to be able to ride. I remember one early morning when I got a phone call from a farmer who lived about fifteen miles north of us to come right away and get our horses, as they were right at the edge of the municipality where there was herd law and no fences to stop them. As soon as animals trespassed into a field of grain, they landed in the pound immediately. We lived in an open district where horses and cattle could run at large; the farmers fenced their crops to protect them from animals. All our menfolk were out threshing way south and I had no time to lose. I ate some breakfast, hurried to the barn, saddled up Punch and we hit the trail. I got to the horses just in time; we had about forty head in the bunch and it would have cost five dollars a head to bail them out if they had been impounded.

Horses are clever animals; they knew us and seemed to know that we were after them. It did not take long to round them up and head them in the right direction for home. We had three distinct families of horses in our bunch. The three old brood mares were the leaders as usual; all of their own offspring would follow them to kingdom come. Whenever we came to a crossroad they split three ways, each taking a different road. Each time we had to run them down and head them back on the right trail. They played with us like this all the way. It was late afternoon when we hit the Ribstone Flat and they were off for Unbuwusts' where there is a grand artesian well. The water runs into a trough continually, so I let them go, thinking that they probably needed a good drink by now and besides, it was only two miles from home. As I rode into the yard behind them I could smell fresh bread baking. This made me real hungry so I tied my horse and asked Grace if she had anything to eat. Needless to say, she fixed me a fine lunch. The horses beat me home and I thought for an instant they looked kind of guilty as Punch and I turned in the gate and sauntered toward the barn.

Chapter XXI

Some of the most enjoyable gatherings we had were the carding parties. Several of our neighbors, as well as ourselves, had a few sheep. Wool was cheap and we hardly knew what to do with it until we hit upon the idea to start making wool quilts. Each one of us sent to a mail order house for a set of carders and in the meantime got the wool washed nice and clean, which in itself is a big job. Since none of us ladies were familiar with the technique of carding, it was a slow process at first and the product of our effort was far from perfect. Then one afternoon one of our bachelor neighbors happened along. He really knew how to card; from then on the men got interested and did most of the carding while we women placed the fluffy batts on the material and tied the quilt. We could finish one by supper time, when a sumptuous meal was set before us. After the dishes were washed and put away, the card tables appeared and bridge began in earnest. This lasted until midnight when the smell of coffee reminded us that the time had come to have some lunch and think about getting home. In the spring we all ended up with a fine lot of nice wool comforters and nothing could compare with the jolly time we had at our carding parties that always ended with cards.

We had rug parties too. Mrs. Banks was the champion rug artist. She taught the rest of us how and many lovely hooked rugs were the result. A lot of men's old wool underwear found its way into these rugs after being dyed a multitude of colors and cut into narrow strips. In fact, our husbands got so suspicious about their underwear disappearing that every time we planned another rug party they pleaded with us, jokingly, not to take the last suit off their backs.

When Chautauqua came to town we could expect the finest in entertainment. This unique travelling show put on two performances a day for four days in succession. The programs were most interesting and varied from comedy to drama, magicians to music. Family tickets were on sale for two dollars and they could be used by any member of the family at all performances. The big hall was crowded to capacity the last evening, when a full length play of some well-known novel was dramatized. One in particular that I remember was "Peg O'My Heart," this being one of the first stage plays that I had ever seen. At the conclusion of the show a dance would wind up the week's activities, the show people joining in the fun with the rest of us. Chautauqua brought us something to remember, to enjoy and relive over and over. Both children and grownups looked forward to next year when they would return once more and bring us another week of enjoyment.

Cold Lake was the fisherman's paradise. Most men looked forward to a week of fishing and hunting in the Fall. The women, also, looked forward to getting some lovely cold lake trout, white fish and pickerel; the latter made the best fish balls imaginable. Then there was generally a moose or deer, depending on the luck of the hunter. I was fortunate in getting in on a trip to this part of Alberta one Fall. Although I did not take part in the sports angle I thoroughly enjoyed the scenery. The pure gold of the native poplars against the intense blue of the lake interspersed here and there with the dark green northern pine was a perfect sight.

Roy had a friend up there by the name of Johnny Johnson. They used to hunt together up around Jackfish Lake where Johnny had a cabin and ran a trapline. One fall they stayed back in the woods for over a month. I was about to report Roy as lost and have the Mounted Police search for him when he rolled in with a load of fish, moose and deer meat and too excited for words over the wonderful experience.

The first two weeks they had no luck whatever. The weather was fine but the game was not to be found. Moose and deer have a keen sense of hearing; the hunter has to step cautiously through the woods so as not to disclose his whereabouts. This is difficult when there is a deep carpet of dry leaves on the ground. They had given up hope and were on their way out when it started to snow so they turned around and went right back. After that they simply lost track of time. When a deep lake begins to freeze over, the temperature in it is warmer than the air around it. This forms a vapor and as soon as the lake freezes over solid, the cloud disappears. The ideal time to hunt big game is right after a light snowfall.

Wainwright Park, or Buffalo Park as we used to call it, was a most unusual attraction for tourists and visitors and a real novelty in itself. In summer we always made it a point whenever possible to pack a big lunch and spend a day in the park. There were upwards of five thousand buffalo roaming around in a twenty-five mile square fenced-in area. That was as much of a natural habitat for the great animal as one could hope to find. This was a government project that originated in 1910 when a herd of buffalo was purchased in the U.S. At first they were considered dangerous and quite a few accidents did occur. Later on they got used to visitors and did not pay very much attention to people. We were warned to stay away during calving season in the spring. There were great numbers of elk, cattalo, yak and antelope all running at large, as well as all kinds of birds, rabbits and, I suspect, the occasional coyote.

I am sure the majority of the citizens of our community regretted very much the decision of the Federal Government of that period to abandon the Park as a buffalo sanctuary and turn it into a rifle range and proving-ground for the armed forces. I, for one, will never get over it.

The United Farmers of Alberta, or U.F.A. organization, played a very important part in the lives of the people of our community. We looked forward to the meetings at the schoolhouse twice a month with interest and enthusiasm. Through it, we had a voice in the affairs of our Province. Hardly a meeting went by without some suggestion or resolution going into central office from our local.

The U.F.A. kept us informed and enlightened on the topics of the day and political aspects of the future. At first we women had joint membership with the men. At times, when we felt like drifting off on some strictly feminine subject like cooking or sewing, we retired to the girls' cloak room. If an issue of importance came up in the men's meeting we were called back in to join in the discussion and vote on the matter. This was a good arrangement and made for a strong organization.

Before long however the women formed their own organization, the U.F.W.A. In summer we met at each other's homes and everyone brought their children along. We got both enjoyment and education from the contacts we made. All our social activities were centered around the U.F.A. We created some really fine entertainments and at one time we had a literary society with two debating teams and two competing newsletters. The Ekrol family contributed a great deal toward our programs; Mrs. Ekrol with her lovely voice and John with his violin. Mr. & Mrs. Witt and their two boys were another talented family and most generous with their musical abilities. The annual picnic on the third of June, as well as the yearly convention at Gooseberry Lake, were also sponsored by the U.F.A.

Another important organization in our community was the Norwegian Ladies Aid. For over twenty years they worked, saved and accumulated enough money to build a church. This was done by having social gatherings on a Sunday once a month at different members' homes, charging only the men twenty-five cents each for the most fabulous lunch, which most of the time included such treats as *lefsa, flatbrod* and *rummegrot,* among a dozen other different varieties of food.

The building of the church was accomplished with the help of much donated labor, not only by members of the Lutheran congregation, but the whole community took pride in the effort and assisted in any way they could. A large warehouse was purchased and dismantled, then rebuilt on several acres of land donated by the Garstad family and stood at the foot of the hills as a symbol of unity, in the form of a lovely church.

Chapter XXII

Farming was getting to be a hit and miss affair. One year we would have a bumper crop and no price; the next year the price would be good but a poor crop and that's the way it went. We had to fall back on our cattle to tide us over from time to time. How we did hate to practically give them away, for the price was next to nothing. I remember one time in particular when we picked out five of our nicest, fattest cows to sell and received sixty dollars for the lot; fifteen hundred pounds at one cent a pound each. When a buyer from the city came around to offer us fifty cents for a good cowhide or two cents a pound for horsehair, we got so we hated the sight of them. Even our dog, a big Russian wolfhound, seemed to sense that they were unwelcome visitors; he would meet them at the gate and just stand there. Not a single one ever tried to get past him. Food was never any problem. We always had plenty to eat and knew how to cook, can, bake and preserve. In fact we practically lived on homegrown food which after all is the very best kind.

We began to hear a lot about the dustbowl in the States and began to fear that it was heading our way, if it hadn't already caught up to us. One dry year after another was beginning to tell on the best of the farmers. Pastures were getting shorter; cattle would dig in and eat old straw piles that they had passed up for years. The stock on the range was getting thin; there were a great number of horses running wild. They did not belong to anyone and were considered a nuisance as well as consuming valuable grass. A roundup was arranged with the aid of the government to get them all together and dispose of them at auction.

Roy and Martin both took part in the roundup. There were close to two hundred head when they were finally brought together and some sold for as little as five dollars. This, I think, was the last roundup of its kind. Horses have been a blessing to humanity through the years. When there was no more money to buy gas, we unbolted the body of the old Ford from the running gear and attached a light wagon tongue by which we changed the horse-power from twenty-two to just two. We went places just the same without license or gas; this was a familiar conveyance and was called the "Bennett Wagon."

It is surprising how resourceful the human race can be if they are compelled. When the crop was too short to harvest in the regular way, the poverty box was invented. This was a square box built on the bundle carrier of the binder. No twine was needed and when the box was full it was dumped in piles on the field to be picked up later and threshed or fed to the stock according to its worth. This was rather slow going for we had a lot of ground to cover. Roy and Martin made a header out of two old binders which enabled them to cut a twelve foot swath. The cut grain was elevated into a large box and when filled it would make a small stack. The tin floor in the bottom, together with a dump truck contraption, enable the straw to slide out and form a neat eight by ten foot stack that could withstand all kinds of weather and was left until the opportune time to thresh.

The barbwire telephone was another hardtime invention. In the outlying districts it was a life-saver. An old-fashioned wall type telephone box cost seven dollars and fifty cents and that was the total expense connected with it. Anyone with a barbwire fence around their place could have a telephone. To get it across the road allowance, a high pole was set up on each side then a wire stretched across and connected to the fence on the other side. Usually the family at the end of the government telephone line had a barbwire telephone also so they could relay messages to town for the doctor in case of sickness or receive telegrams and announcements from town to the people on the barbwire line who couldn't be notified otherwise. Mr. & Mrs. Hailstone had such an arrangement. I am sure there are many people grateful for their kindness in relaying calls. It was also a source of entertainment; when the radio was first introduced not many had the means with which to buy one. Those neighbors who did were very accommodating and would call everybody on the line to listen to the lovely music, for hours at a time.

The Beef Ring was a really clever system of having fresh meat in the summer. About twenty families belonged to our Ring; each one contributed a nice steer when their turn came. One man did all the killing and delivery for a small sum. The animal was divided into twenty parts and each family got a different part every Saturday. At the end of the twenty weeks we had received one whole animal. The numbers from one to twenty were placed in a hat and whichever number you drew was your week to have your steer ready to butcher. It made no difference whether it weighed fourteen hundred or one thousand pounds, it was divided equally according to its weight. Beef was so cheap it was not worth quarrelling over.

Every little community had its picnic. A special date was set for each, every year. Avonlea was no exception; this was their day for the annual get-together. Instead of a big folks' competition in sports, a school children's baseball tournament was the attraction of the day. The children were anxious to go, especially since the Veteran boys' team had entered. I volunteered to take as many as I could in our car. There was real excitement, for the children had been granted a half holiday from classes and were confident of victory, since their team was considered one of the best.

Some of the players were already on the field warming up as we landed. The rest of our boys were right behind us and we heard the familiar shout "Play ball" from the umpire. Everybody lined up to root for their own team and exchange genial guff, as usual. The folks from the hills were all there and others from different localities gathered around to join in on the friendly banter typical at a country picnic.

It was a perfect day for sports, sunny and warm with not a breath of air stirring. We needed rain; the crops looked stunted and blighted and we were forever looking for a cloud that would bring us some relief from the drought. The excitement was great; our boys were in the lead. Suddenly there was something about the atmosphere that made me feel uneasy. I noticed little puffs of wind twirl the dust into miniature whirlwinds and carry them across the field. One raised on the prairie develops a certain intuition or instinct about the weather. I soon noticed a few dark clouds in the west. They rose swiftly and had a peculiar dark current through them and before long, as I feared, had gathered into a funnel-like shape and grew with amazing rapidity, soon blotting out the sun and darkening the sky. A dead calm that was terrifying was felt by us all. Sports and activities stopped and all eyes turned in the direction of the storm; we knew what was coming.

I was the first to break the silence with "Come on, boys, run for the car, we are hitting for home." The girls were already waiting. We lost no time in getting away, amid protests of some old timers, who thought it safer to stay where we were. Although the storm was bearing down on us rapidly, I hoped to make the six miles to town before it caught up with us. The wind was at our back, which was in our favor, at least.

As we started out, Fred Davis, who was on foot, came running and panting, "Gee, lady, I know you have a car full, but could you possibly stuff me in?" "Sure, Fred, climb in." He quickly closed the door and we were off. We hardly dared look behind us. A black wall was descending upon us, blotting out the scenery. Where half an hour ago it had been bright sunshine, darkness now befell us and I turned on the car lights. Armies of Russian thistle came rolling across the prairie; many of these huge balls of nasty prongs, some as large as buggy wheels, caught in the barb-wire fences and accumulated there until it looked like a hedge and enabled the rest to roll right over and pollute the countryside with millions of seed.

I had to let Fred out at his gate. With the brake to the floor, the car rolled on several yards before it slowed up enough for him to jump out. We got three miles further down the road before the storm really stopped us. The dense mass of swirling, choking dust seemed to envelop us. We could not see a foot ahead; only at times could I make out the top of the telephone poles on the side of the road allowance. We would then inch our way a few feet and stop; thus we continued to creep along. The dust penetrated the car, nearly choking us and covering everything with a thick blanket of black dirt, in spite of tightly rolled-up windows.

It took us two hours to make the last three miles. When we finally made it home, there were several anxious mothers waiting. Everything in the house was covered with dust an inch thick. The storm kept on for several hours, still it brought no rain. It was heart-breaking to look at the fields of grain, hundreds of acres uprooted. What was left standing was bedraggled and sickly looking. Drifts of dust had piled along fence lines where cattle could walk right over them in places. Some fields were swept clean, surface soil blowing here and there, piled up to await the next windstorm to blow it back and forth again. Roy was plowing when the storm hit. He shut off the tractor, left the plow in the ground, climbed down and wrapped his sweater over his head and lay flat on the ground until the worst was over; that was the sensible thing to do.

The drought kept on. Some families were in real distress; there was no organized system of relief at the time so we helped each other the best we could. One fall the farmers of Ontario sent a carload of vegetables, apples and clothing to our town to be distributed among the needy; the railroad hauled it free of charge. There were also a lot of nice wool blankets included from some woollen mills, which was a wonderful gesture and helped a lot of people. The district south of town was the worst off. The grasshoppers added to their plight and stripped all vegetation, even to digging down to get at the roots of the rhubarb plants. We were more fortunate up north; somehow we managed to grow a pretty good garden and some crop. At least we managed to get our seed back in the Fall.

When the lean years hit us we did not sit home and cry on each other's shoulders; we had our weekly dance just the same. We found that we could have just as good a time with less money, if we were willing to give of ourselves a little. We had the same musicians in the community; quite a few of the boys could play the violin some and were encouraged to practise more and help out with the music. It seems almost impossible when I think of the dances we kept on having every Friday night. No orchestra was engaged ahead of time or lunch provided for except voluntary contributions. Someone brought coffee and floor wax and we hoped that the ten cent collection taken up would be sufficient to cover that and the gas for the lamps. No one had to contribute or stay at home because of lack of funds; only those who felt they could afford it paid the dime.

Different ones took turns about being responsible for putting on the next dance. They were the ones to get there first, light the lamps, clear the floor of school desks and sprinkle the wax. Everybody brought something, those who had musical instruments and could play were sure to bring them along. Several could chord on the piano and they would change off from time to time. The same old cake pans were lined up on the shelf as in more prosperous times, with the same good cakes. Instead of the huge box of sandwiches we used to order from Suey, the Chinaman in town, there were many small boxes of homemade ones. The ladies knew what kind each was to bring so as to have a variety. Each family took its turn to stay and clean the school after the dance, for the floor had to be scrubbed, desks replaced and everything left in order for school the next Monday. If there happened to be any money left over after taking out for coffee, floor wax and gas, it was saved for the next dance and so we carried on until better times came along again.

As baby sitters were unheard of in those days we all brought our children along. They looked forward to the weekly dance with as much enthusiasm as the grown people and would have suffered immensely if they had been made to stay home. The little ones slept through it all in their baskets. The others would sit, watch and listen to the music, with never a peep out of them, until they got too sleepy and had to be bedded down. The ones old enough to dance (and that was as soon as they started to school) would have a dance played just for them, every so often. It was fun to watch the little fellows and bigger ones too run across the floor to ask the little girls in the nicest manner, "Please, may I have this dance?" This was part of their training for the future. The floor manager saw to it that the boys did escort their partners to their seats when the dance finished and say, "Thank you for the nice dance." For supper waltz there was a lively competition among the youngsters to get the girl of his choice to eat lunch with him.

Chapter XXIII

The trek of the dried-out farmers and ranchers from the south of town had begun; wagon loads and hayracks full of belongings passed by our place every few days. Usually there were two wagons. The man would be in the lead with a four-horse team on the hayrack loaded with the most necessary household furniture and machinery piled together; the mower and rake tied behind. These were most essential. The wife would be close behind with two horses to a wagon. In it would be dishes, silver, linen and bedding, food and a chest of drawers or trunks with what valuables they possessed, a crate or two of chickens and the house cat in her crate, which turned out to be a humpty-dumpty egg crate. A few milk cows, herded by a kid or two on horseback, would follow and the extra workhorses would trail. Occasionally they would stop and eat when they found a bit of good grass but would run to catch up before the outfit went out of sight, as if they were afraid to be left behind. The family dog was trotting along, seldom barking at anything, intent upon catching every gopher along the road, as well as keeping the cows from straying off.

This was a familiar sight and quite often they used to stop and water their animals and camp for the night at our place. These people were not looking for sympathy and we knew enough not to offer any. The look in their eyes was not one of defeat but of new hope. Rather than lose everything they pulled up stakes and left the place they had worked so hard to develop from a piece of raw prairie into a lovely farm, only to have it turn into a shifting desert. In the morning, when they were ready to hit the road, I would wrap up a couple of loaves of home-made bread to give her. She only said "Thank you" but the look in her eyes haunted me; I only hoped a similar fate wouldn't be my lot. Not that I was afraid, for I had done it before, but in my mind I argued against it and as she drove away I just stood there and repeated over and over "Please, God, let it rain!"

When drought has taken over, there is not much one can do to combat it. We had many years of it in succession and it was beginning to tell on all of us. The land was parched, the pastures bare and the prairie grass was so dry and brittle that it crushed under our feet and left a footprint, as if we had stepped in sand. Roy had dust pneumonia in the Fall and rheumatism all Winter. His Dad came up from Maryland again in the Spring to pay us a visit and persuaded Roy to go back home with

him for a rest and vacation. This was July; the children and I were holding forth by ourselves. Florence and Harry Dunn, two neighbor children
who made their home with us off and on for several years, were with us
also. The heat was scorching during the daytime; every day we searched
the intense blue sky for some sign of a cloud that might give us some
hope of a shower. I kept the children in the cellar; this was a full basement, the only difference was that the walls were of blue clay instead of
concrete. I spread a rug on the floor and brought them lunch and plenty of water to drink and they played down there until evening.

The nights were comfortable and it was cool after sundown. The
heat wave lasted for two weeks; when the rain finally came it was as if
the heavens opened up and poured it on us. We all ran out in it and got
good and wet; the animals, too, just stood where they were and let it soak
in. I have never seen rain come down so fast before. Our front yard had
four inches of water standing on the level before it had time to run off.
The peculiar thing about this shower, and that which interested me
most, was that all the people who were fortunate enough to have been
in the path of the rain did the same as we did: stood out in it and got a
good soaking.

When Roy came home he was all for us moving to Maryland.
He had felt much better while there and thought the milder climate
would help him regain his health. We did not however want to burn the
bridges behind us altogether, so we decided to keep our land and enough
equipment so we would have something to start with, in case we wanted to come back again. This made me feel more secure. I knew from
experience that it is not altogether sunshine-and-roses to leave one's
home and go to a strange country to live. Homesickness and that lonesome feeling is bound to come no matter what you do before one
becomes acclimated and feel as though you really belong.

We had our sale and disposed of everything, including the live-
stock. It was sad to see our lovely horses trot over the hill for the last
time. Next morning, when Roy went down to the barn to milk the cow,
which had been left by the man who bought her so we would have milk
for the children until we were ready to go, what should be standing in
the stall waiting for his oats but my Billy Boy. The door had been left
open for the cow to roam at large since she was the only animal still on
the place. We hadn't seen Billy for years; the last we had heard of him,
Ole had lent him to a family south of town for a school pony. They did-
n't bring him back so we thought he must have died. Roy thought he

recognized him but wasn't sure, for he was getting old and quite thin. I hurried down to the barn and knew him right away. I walked up to him and punched him gently in the ribs like I used to when he was young and I was a kid and he nipped me on the sleeve in the same old manner. We let him stay all day and fed him all we thought was good for him. Then in the evening Roy took him down home and turned him out. The strange thing is that after we were married, he was never at our place more than a day at a time. It seemed like he sensed in some way that I was leaving and he wanted to have the last visit with me.

We were to leave the next day. The few belongings we had left after the sale were barely enough to camp overnight with; these were to be stowed away in the cabin we had reserved for ourselves to be used whenever we happened to be back for a visit. About eight o'clock that night our friends and neighbors began to roll in and before long the house was packed. Lack of conveniences and facilities made no difference; the men brought in chunks of wood and long boards to make seats for the older ones to sit on. The rest of us either danced or played games; everyone had a fine time. We cooked coffee on the heating stove and the ladies had brought everything for a fine lunch. The party lasted until midnight, when one by one they departed for home.

Our farewell party was over, the last visitor had gone; what a hilarious time we all had! Every one did his utmost to make it a success. We all felt that strange feeling, though, and it was worse when we shook hands and said goodbye. Tears seemed to find their way, even among the men, no matter how hard we tried to keep them back, for they were all our friends, real friends. We had grown up together, gloried in each other's achievements, suffered the same setbacks and laughed at fate in the same manner when the old elf stacked the cards against us.

When all was quiet and the rest had gone to bed, I put on Roy's sheepskin coat and ventured out for a breath of fresh air. I walked to the top of the hill behind the house. It was late November, the night air was cold, it felt good against my face. Even the atmosphere seemed a bit sad; the sky was thick, a big ring encircled the moon; it was evident that a storm was in the air. The wind whistling down from the hills whispered a warning of snow. Old Dutty, the cat, rubbed against me as if to comfort me and the dogs, puzzled at me venturing out so late, sat faithfully by, shivering a little. All nature seemed to understand. The hills were barely visible, snow-covered and silent. "I am going away," I heard myself saying, "not for always. I'll be back."

Epilogue

The last half century has seen a multitude of changes. Not so long ago, as I was winging my way from coast to coast in a very few hours aboard a jet airliner, I couldn't help but think back to the days of the prairie schooner. I seemed to feel the shake of the wagon as it followed the dim trail across the prairie; and thinking back, it was a good life. We took it in stride in those days, the pace was a bit slow compared to the present. This gave us the opportunity to gaze at the surrounding territory and see what was going on. When the plane landed, and it was a perfect landing, it dawned on me that I had seen nothing but fleecy clouds. I am glad that I have had the privilege of rolling along life's highway slowly enough to observe what lies ahead and at the sides of the road. The view was not always grand or picturesque; one has to take the bad with the good as we travel along.

We have now been established citizens for many years on the lovely eastern shore of Maryland, in the friendly town of Federalsburg. If there is such a thing as a dual citizen, I must be one. I get the same thrill listening to "America, the Beautiful" as I do "O Canada" and if the occasion should call for the national anthem of Norway, I can join with the same feeling. One never forgets one's mother tongue.

Pioneering is now a thing of the past, as we knew it. This story is written with the idea in mind of preserving the true experiences of the early days for future generations, that they might appreciate the efforts of their forefathers who blazed the trail. Also to prove that it is not luxuries and conveniences that make for a full life. It is that which we have within us that counts. Love and determination will conquer most of the difficulties of life, if we put them to work.